*"Holistic Spiritual Approach on Magical Module"*
VJOLLCA SADIKU
Co- Founder & Director
Magical Coaching

# "Power of Pure Love..."

*"Practicing Purity Teaches you Self-Love... Permanent Happiness and Contribute to Creating a Peaceful and Loving World "*

## Education Book

*Vjollca Sadiku*

SH.B
Lena

**Gotham Books**
30 N Gould St.
Ste. 20820, Sheridan, WY 82801
https://gothambooksinc.com/

Phone: 1 (307) 464-7800

Published by Gotham Books (July 15, 2022)

ISBN: 978-1-956349-96-2 (sc)
ISBN: 978-1-956349-97-9 (e)

Because of the dynamic nature of the Internet, any web addresses or links contained in this book may have changed since publication and may no longer be valid.

The views expressed in this work are solely those of the author and do not necessarily reflect the views of the publisher, and the publisher hereby disclaims any responsibility for them.

Prepared and designed by Lena Graphic Prishtine.

Seven Stages Of Holistic Magical Approach Module:

 MOMENTUM

 ACCEPTANCE

 GOAL

 INSPIRATION

 COMMITMENT

 AFFIRMATION

LOVE

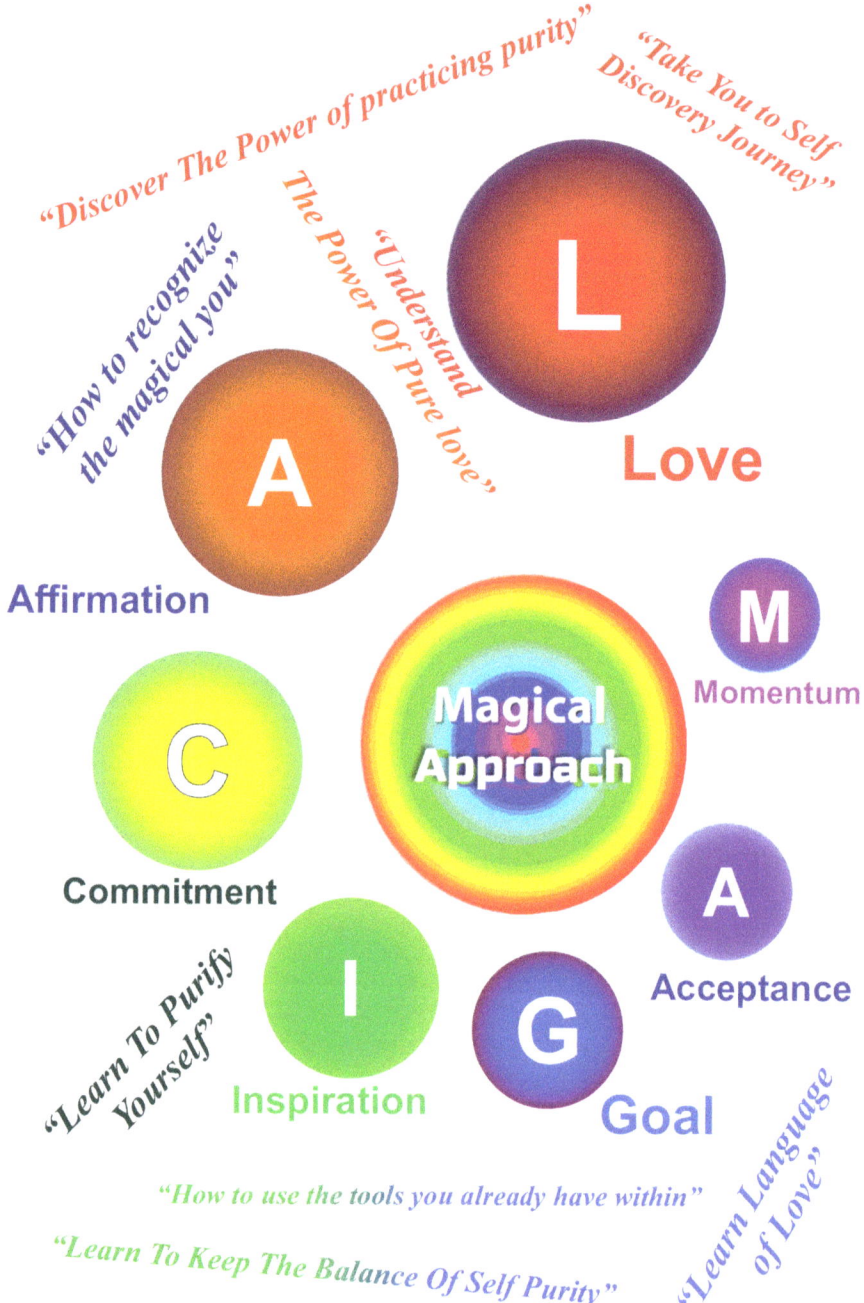

"Discover The Power of practicing purity"

"Take You to Self Discovery Journey"

"How to recognize the magical you"

"Understand The Power Of Pure love"

**L** Love

**A** Affirmation

**M** Momentum

**C** Commitment

**Magical Approach**

**A** Acceptance

"Learn To Purify Yourself"

**I** Inspiration

**G** Goal

"How to use the tools you already have within"

"Learn Language of Love"

"Learn To Keep The Balance Of Self Purity"

4

# PREFACE

This book will help you to connect with your inner self, be resilient, find your purpose, defeat distraction, and feel content in life. Are you ready to start living your dream life today? Be happy all the times here and now? And contribute to creating a peaceful and loving world?

## Educational Book

Seven programs how to live a peaceful and loving life here and now: Gain self-love, take action based on guidance of your true self, learn how to live a life guided by your soul and intuition and learn how to keep balance of your whole you (mind, heart, body, soul and intuition).

Benefits of those achievements are to overcome any illness, trauma, difficulties, relationship confusions, loneliness, be the best you can be in your job, help others in right direction, suicide thoughts, self-harm, addictions, achieving your full potential and basically anything that you are struggling or getting on the way of being happy, fulfilled and loved here and now.

Note: Who copy my methods will just make their journey harder as it can not be taught by person who has not gained self-love (be guided by their soul and intuition) ....and the person who has gained self-love will never copy because they will have their own mind ....their own way to share with others ......

Where I got the learning of self-love and how I come up with Magical Module....look at my first book " A Magical Life " "To gain self-love means being guided all the time by your soul and intuition " ....

In order to teach Magical model you have to be trained by Holistic Spiritual Magical Approach Module.

# CONTENTS

6

"Holistic Spiritual Approach on Magical Module"

VJOLLCA SADIKU
Co- Founder & Director
Magical Coaching

# 111

# Life learning Quotes

# 111 Life learning Quotes:

1- "Life is Magical...You are Magical.....because life is adventures, growth, joy, and you are the master of life "

2- "You are created from energy...You are energy....soul"

3- "Your intuition is the voice of your creator"

4- "Your life is based on your actions and decisions"

5- "You are in this life to enjoy life and share love with others"

6- "Loving yourself is the only thing you have to achieve...because the rest will follow"

7- "If you don't love yourself you can not love others because you don't know yet what love is"

8- "If you want the best for someone, why you will feel disappointed if they don't treat you well? If you want their best all it matter is for them to be doing well for themselves....... so your disappointment may come from your hidden purpose of wanting something from them....need to learn more about yourself"

9- "If you believe in the creator and yourself ..... why should you find your life path difficult and painful to achieving your goals? ..... change the purpose or look at yourself ..... !! ... because the life journey should feel adventurers if you really believe in yourself and creator......
hurt happens because you want things ready from others ..... "

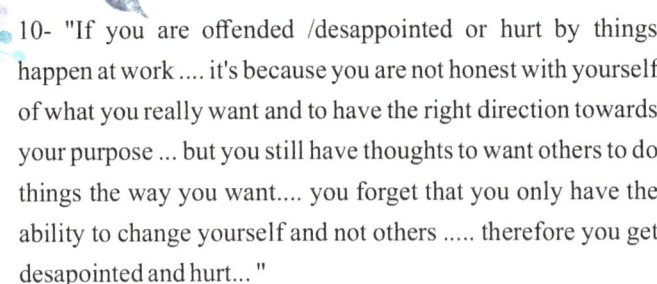

10- "If you are offended /desappointed or hurt by things happen at work .... it's because you are not honest with yourself of what you really want and to have the right direction towards your purpose ... but you still have thoughts to want others to do things the way you want.... you forget that you only have the ability to change yourself and not others ..... therefore you get desapointed and hurt... "

11- "If you getting hurt by people who you live with ...... then you are still thinking of having things as you want and changing the other .... and not doing the right thing by yourself and the other...... and this is where the air of the smoke of irritation is blown ..... because the purpose you have chosen to live with that person has not been based on purity, kindness and love ... but in control of other and changing things that are not based in your responsibility...... "

12- "As a parent if you getting hurt by your children behaviours .... it because you are not clear on your role as parent and the purpose of being a parent ....to become a parent is the miracle and is the most precious work that exists in this life ... .. also the hardest work because it is forming an individual ..... the individual who will be happy for themselves and contribute to a world of being in peace and love...... if as parent you remembers this purpose then there is no hurt or problems but only the solutions ....... that's why is important to have only "love", "sense", "listening", "exploring ideas and techniques based on pure love " and working as a parent should be the goal primary of life if you have decided to be a parent ....... "

13. "If you do not have enough money for what you need....it means that you do not believe in your skills and are not using your skills ..."

9

14. "If you do not feel satisfied… is because you don't love yourself… and don't appreciate what you have."

15. "There are moments that you feel empty …. it's because you do not pay attention to the desires and do not plan to achieve the dreams/wishes …"

16. "It seem like no-one understands you and you try to please others … it's because you hate yourself and do not like who you are …."

17. "It seems like others do injustice to you and you are trying to persuade them to change …it is because you are doing injustice towards yourself and others" …."

18. "If the world seems difficult…. it is because you are not taking time to understand your inner world …..yourself "

19. " Feel disappointed !!! …. it is because you expects things from others …. and underestimates yourself …. is lacking in self-confidence and self belive to achieve things on your own"

20. "Feelings of suffering … it is because you are at the level of the heart and mind …. you have to connect with the soul to understand your heart and mind ….. the soul does not feel the suffering because it is love"

21. "You have physical pain … it is because you have ignored the internal voice and the body is suffering from pains ….is calling you to hear yourself;"

22. "If Time is not enough for you … it's because you spend it where is not need it..... need to learn to manage it :)"

23. "All that is needed in this life is self-love to live in peace, love, and reach the material world you need"

24. "If the parent has not achieved self-love .... there is no way to teach the child self-love"

25. "I take care of myself to live today and have the ability to build and make better tomorrow"

26. "What is left is the sensation of the moment ...the feeling of pure love… any sensation that comes for future moments should be better then what it was, because we grow as we live... this is called the practice of everlasting happiness"

27. "Life is a mystery ... that just by being sure about the choices of the moment, you can explore and enjoy ... this is called happiness"

28. "The love of the moment is our essence ... it is all that matters if it is related to the vision of the future"

29. "Nothing hurts us if we do not allow it"

30. "Everything is exalted with the divine love that we have within if it has been written to be healed and if it is stronger than the fear"

31. "Happiness stems from consciousness ... from spiritual and psychological abilities ... and being aware is a process; is a journey ... "

32. "Happiness, peace, love and harmony exists within... and not in the place we choose to live or in a place where we from ... "

33. "If fear does not exist in unknown things.... it means that you are not doing things with your full consciousness....
(mind, body, heart, soul and intuition)" ...

34. "It is good when you work towards your plans ........ because it helps your growth, expands the horizon for more information to help me be in the right path, right time..... Grow more spiritually and have clear way to the vision "

35. "Who believes in righteousness and justice ....in purity… it is never disappointment ... but rather a challenge, an upsurge and a raise ... everything is a win situation .... even when you fall or get hurt..... because you can see beyond what is presented and therefore rises up and moves for a better purpose and pleasure... "

36. "Your thoughts are like the paintbrush of an artist. They create your own image of the reality of each moment…. so choose the colours you like to use and be clear of the vision of painting you like to paint. "

37. "If we are angry or frustrating by the other is our fault and not the other" ....

38. "The individual must find harmony and pleasure and then be able to see clearly outwardly"

39. "We forget to understand that we are really happy where we are ..here and now... we simply confuse happiness with desires ... desires do not bring us happiness ....."

40. "If we are not happy here and now …..even tomorrow we will not know how to be happy"

41. "No one is perfect but we just try to make ourselves happy and understand how to live life in peace and love without being influenced by others and the outside world ...... this journey is unique to everybody and mysterious "

42. "No one is stupid or bad ... but our decisions and actions make us bad and stupid ... take us away from ourselves .... because we are all good and unique"

43. "If you are in the moment ... you never regret the past ....
you just learn, laugh and smile again"

44. "Understanding the peace of love must believe in nothingness ...
in the existence of the Beauty of feeling that is not confirmed
but only felt"

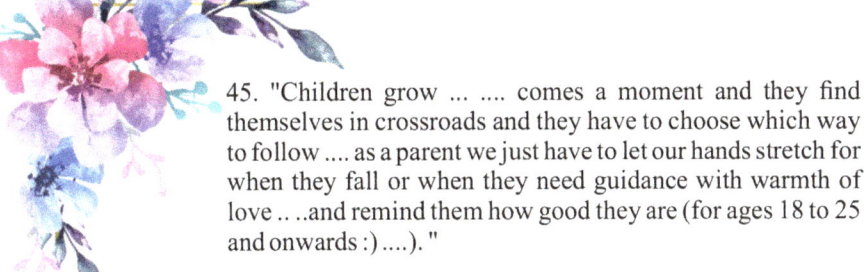

45. "Children grow ... .... comes a moment and they find themselves in crossroads and they have to choose which way to follow .... as a parent we just have to let our hands stretch for when they fall or when they need guidance with warmth of love .. ..and remind them how good they are (for ages 18 to 25 and onwards :) ....). "

46. "Children around the ages of 11 to 16 Are really very different and creative .... the age that needs the guidance of adults without prejudice but with lots of pure love and the exploration of their creativity"

47. "The past is the lesson I am who I am ... The present is what embraces the past, builds the future and lives the moment .... The future is unknown"

48. "A person who is satisfied with themself and life always speaks with love, kindness, and justice towards themself and others"

49. " Who is unhappy with themselves and their lives are not using the language of love to speak with themselves and others"

50. "We have everything we need and don't need nothing from outside world ... except to share what we have ..... "

51. "A person who is not satisfied and does not feel in peace and love with themself, life and others ......can do harm to themself and others...... "

52. "Being self aware of the things we don't like for oneself and others is a step towards the implementation of goodness and justice to oneself and others"

53. "To lead our life by our soul (the pure part that exists in each of us ... in the form of energy or feeling ... the part we are in the truth and that part is that never dies ...) and intuition (the voice of creator's) Taking care of the mind, the heart, and the body makes us live a life full of love and harmony ..... without the pain and the problems ...... but where there is only solution, pleasure, peace and love "

54.. " Happiness comes within.... the individual is born with a sense of happiness .... we must use it during the life journey growth in order to maintain it"

56."After all the love ... after all the hurt .... after every wave .... the calmness of the water comes with the sunlight" (.all happen for a reason ...  clean energy and  be ready for something new) "

57. "To passionately love a person with a purity means to want their happens not to aspect things from them.....but share love you both have" (so I say self-love first and then comes universal love and in the end the passionate love ....... after you have learned to live in peace and love) "

58. "From the hurtful feelings we learn the most valuable lessons on how to enlighten more ....."

59. "From failures .... we can raise higher then before if we take the learning from it"

60. "Where we think that there is injustice, we must express our opinion or not be part of that injustice"

61. "Moment is all I need .... in many cases we forget to stop asking" what do we really want from this moment and how can we use the moment with a balance where 5% learn from the past, 80% enjoy the present with whatever we choose to do and 15% to work towards the future ......... total falls to 100% to do in the present exactly what we enjoy and what serves us for the future "

62. "Everyone is born awake and during growth we forget to hear ourselves, but fill ourselves with information from the outside world ........we get lost on those informations because is no sense of pure love in the information from outside world"

63. "Nothing happens by chance, we must be vigilant to understand this chronology of things ..."

64 "Who overcome suffering are wiser, who is raised with love and used their creativity for their own happiness and to serve others are wiser..... but who get stuck between those two journeys is stuck need guidance to follow their own path .."

65. "Whoever seeks the truth ....will find it and feel it.... because the truth is feeling ... same as faith and pure love " ...

66. "To be good person ...it means to be happy with everything you do all the times....because you know what you like and what you don't like .....you are in charge of the decision's and choices" ...

67. " Never feel guilty about the way you feel.... embrace it, learn and keep swimming in love"

68. "Trusting the inner guidance is an unknown road.... but is the right road"

69. "Working with children is the most rewarding job because you will get in touch with your side of purity that exist inside you"

70. "Being you is all you need ___ being in love is next step to fly in love ____ to be a parent is the best thing can ever happen to you ___ to enjoy what you have is the success and meaning of life ____ to see your children grow into happy adults is most rewarding thing you can receive from the work you have put into life ___ to be able to contribute into the world for a peaceful and loving energy is our last duty to fulfil our journey of this life ___ Life is Magical.... You are Magical "

71. "When you follow the flow of your inner guidance.....you will look crazy, wired or strange to outer world ....but need to remind yourself .......who feels good....you or those that see you as weird and as crazy person !!!?....once you answer this question then you know what is the right path....because all we want is to feel good ...;) and enjoy here and now ....but if we can't achieve that for ourselves then is likely people around as to be different from what we are ;) "

72. "Inner guidance from mind and heart only can be use to you ....to help you understand yourself and your journey so far and why you are unhappy....and lots more ....but they are not the right guidance to take you where you want to be ....to the place where you feel happy here and now and have clear plan about future......the inner guidance from your soul and intuition are pure and the guidance you have to trust .....and that's what my programmes meant to achieve ...which is called self-love coming from base of purity.....soul and intuition "

73. "We should not be scared of death or what others do to us because our light still will be on .....we should be scared of doing wrong to ourselves and others because that will make us be in dark ........being in light means you are happy exactly where you are and you have clear plan for future....also you never hurt yourself or others .......being in dark means it does not matter how good your reality is ...you still not satisfied and feel that emptiness inside you ...which lead to doing wrong to yourself and others "

74. "Home for me is a feeling....and it is here in this life....
Of course not around people that don't practice purity.....
I call that work with passion .....But home for me is a feeling fulfilled, in peace and loved here and now "

75. " Life is good... Self-love is real you that gives you everything what you need ...universal love is about sharing and having fun as we grow...(family, friends and others in our life)...passionate love is the end of destination on searching .....is to lay back and enjoy the sunshine....as in autopilot you do the rest "

76."Being fully in moment you don't remember things that don't serve your purpose....because you have to be in empty space in order to alloy yourself to hear unseen information's ....you need room to receive new information in relaxed way"

77. "To be responsible. If once, my responsibility was to remain silent, with the same ideas in my head, today I have to reflect, think, discuss and feel the weight of things and the role in this weight..." client said..

78. "Facing the situation, when one has someone who they consider as a guide in life, brings a sense of security, one is obedient to their mission..."

79." I can get out of the no-return situation where I was (with distorted dreams, of a difficult life without a way out)" client said...

80. "The connection with the soul is more difficult but it is achievable. For me it is an inner voice that constantly calls, although we hear it in a hurry" clients said...

81." All is complicated and need lots of work but all it starts by going back before we decided to come to rise life- to soul- to creator -to universe- and main ingredients are pure, determination, creativity, curiosities. ...

Your answer is based on how connected you are with your soul ......how often you stay in that energy. .... can you recognise your voices in your head...... which level is your heart and mind. ....then how much you know about your purpose. ....how pure you are and what you have done so far ...etc etc ....

Karma. ..law of attraction. ...your faith on your self and creator etc"

82." Individual in bauble of life- outside the life - universe, creator, purpose, why we are in this life - we born and die- understanding body, mind, heart, soul- crave for love - but don't know the meaning of love - read books, learn from others but we forget that everything is within and we have to make decisions within in order to be us and serve our purpose. Our reasons from coming to this life- we never questions why we come to this life - what is love – "

17

83. "It was a world where things were smaller than the size I had given them (problems) It was a more detailed analysis of the action, but the actions did not happen and they had a guilty taste, but the situation had to be analysed Everything that I was trying to connect to the soul and everything I was living with the universe and my soul, at that time it was the currents that make you to be optimistic today was a wider border, a clear dimension to a new self ... without deep understanding and things went into analysis then the analysis could fade because of the impossibility of spiritual fulfilment and blocked by shadows, fear of reality to Love yourself ... A new meaning to love it, that makes you understand more things and the relationships with the soul continued as often until things were clarified, the universe provided many details, made to look differently and to believe to on soul and universe". Said it by the client.

84. "To live with the soul… you have heard but is far in distance ... you heard in the dream of the vision that there is an ivory thread that needs to be understood, the faces were elusive, the horizons of a riot that was in the mind. there are a lot of things you've been wondering, what to bother and what you've understood before ... was a situation that seemed to reflect only in books but in reality it was in the corner, in that corner that you have it looks like a upsetting place, where your self has always been a wintering project, It happens without understanding, I had spiritual guidance, but it was disconnection because a new person was regenerating. " said it by the client.

85." By loving yourself and everything on earth, you attract the same loving energy, which leads to living in a magical place. Love is the cure of life and the heart is that special place where you receive all your answers. True and powerful love begins within you."

86." Remember to praise yourself about your goodness and the great abilities you possess. Congratulate your whole being for the amazing things you are doing to fulfill your life's purpose. Keep nurturing yourself. Be specific in your words of praise and wishes towards the universe, is nothing wrong with asking for help."

18

87." Be a good listener to the inner guidance, all your senses, and nature. By trusting the laws of the universe, you give" yourself adequate time to practice intuition and spontaneity for aligning with your purpose, when the time is right. Have conversations with your thoughts, organize them, embrace them, ask questions, discuss your answers, reflect on your decisions, allow yourself to feel your feelings and remember the reason of doing what you are doing; think whether you still want it...if not, allow yourself to change things... If you do not feel like changing, because you need more motivation then the next stage will help you with that.

88." Remember to pause and notice the amazing things around. Inspiration can be found anywhere and in anything that surrounds you, good or bad, is always something to spark your imagination and fire your creativity. Every step has its own challenges but inspiration is like a fresh breeze for your mind and soul. It maintains the passion and love for the goal and helps you to continue enjoying the journey. "

89." "The magic of life lies in your soul, where it finds the purity of pure love ... where there is only goodness ... where love is produced" (so whoever are religion leaders or people who represent themselves as good persons, you can feel it through the silence. ... the energy is in that moment ... "The sun can warm you up with the lights he has and you are not able to look at straight on with eyes because we are not pure as human .... is the same way when you look people on the eye ...you can tell so much about it if you just let the silence guide you")."

90." Love yourself, life, others, and everything that surrounds you ... this is the meaning of life ... this is the disappearance of dissatisfaction ... this is the disappearance of complaints ... this is the love without limitations .... free love ....magic love that creates magic on you and the life you are surrounded. "

91." In order to know what is best for others first you have to know what is good for you"

19

92." The law of the universe is simple, you simply need to be pure and want justice for yourself and others. You have to show compassion, understanding, care and love towards you as a whole and others as a whole."

93." Learn to accept and love yourself for who you are and the way you are. Analyse what you do not like about yourself and plan how you're going to change or make improvements. Alternatively, you can accept these flaws and not complain about them."

94." Believe in your uniqueness and the universe will guide you. Remember if you can't accept and love yourself just the way you are you will not have confidence, high self esteem and have lots of doubts, you are not sure that you deserve what your vision is."

95." *Personality* is the same for those who are guided by the soul. Only their journey will be different. For those who will be guided by their mind and heart their personality will be different because will be mixed up with thoughts and feelings as explained in momentum stage from the reality and others. "

96." *Depression from the soul* is for those who are guided by the soul. This category enjoys this kind of depression because is all about serving their mission to study in depth things with pleasure. Once you reach this stage you are not attached to the outside world but you master it and enjoy it also you become a great teacher to others around you. "

97." *Depression from the heart* is a deep depression and is not healthy if not dealt with. This type of depression usually happens to those people who are guided the most from their feelings, from their heart. But if is dealt as explained through stages of magical model is the bridge to the soul, to your true self."

98." *Mild Depression* is something all people who are not guided by their soul experience and deal with due to a lack of a connection with their soul."

99." Live for yourself ... or do not blame someone else because I'm sure there are options to protect you. .... when you are pure, determined and resilient in searching what you want, the creator and universe is with you and will help you ."

100." *Soul relationship is when you only connect through soul but don't agree with each other's actions and thoughts. Human relationship is when you know each other very well including mind, heart and as whole. To be able to recognise*

*those two types of relationship you have self-love first and understanding of universal love then you ar ready for relationship. "*

101." The breathing needs to be practiced, that by breathing you can go to the soul and contact with creator for guidance. "

102." Remember, remember and remember. You were born alone in this world and for a purpose. You are special, remember to believe in your light: your purpose. Remember you know why you came into this life journey. Simply go deeper into depth, going beyond your being and being one with your soul. There you will be full of strength, love, and you see that everything is happening for something better."

103." True love. It is when we fall in love with the soul of the person and he has created his life based on the soul guidance, so mind and heart are meant to serve the soul. So we have to look at th individual as whole. The mind and heart must be combined to a level with the soul."

104." The difference between the soul and the creators is that the creator has wider knowledge, but the knowledge of the soul comes from knowledge of your life purpose and previous life experiences. Do we need to know how to recognize our soul, starting from the very essence of his existence? Through the spirit we can change our thoughts and leave behind those we do not need. How can we allow the spiral of the spirit to guide us, given that the soul is close to creator, innocent and always right"

105." The soul is as something internal, and all of the importance lies in our theories, our doings, our acting on things in three dimensions:

Saying – what I don't believe, but that I want to happen.
Do-as well as I think (without realizing that I don't understanding what I am doing.)
Acting - another form that neither the saying and doing does not match and do not have the benefit of acting and saying as they don't correspond." Said by client.

106." "When you do not know yourself ... you do not have the ability to know the creator either",

107." Relationships in the family, mother, father, sister, brother and other members a big family is part of universal love. If a person has not achieved self-love, then they will follow their path because they need universal love and they will be dependent on them.

Universal love is simply survival but nothing else, so survival in the wrong way, breathing without realizing why you are and what is your path and why you really exists. If you love your family, you need to find the way to win love for yourself. If you do not find self-love you end up hurting them and your self. If you win your love for yourself, then your life becomes meaningful, and you enjoy life, then you can understand and enjoy the love of the family. "

108." Understand your reason for this life, Believe in your skills, speak up the truth, do what you really want to do based on purpose and you are always in a position to implement your thoughts in collaboration with creator and your soul."

109. "Love to yourself ... I... How am I .... Am I...Perseverance...Trust ..Internal...Force ... motive ...Freedom ...Clear...Sincerity (communication or loving someone with out intrest)....Study (deepening not with the monotony) ....Look as whole picture: I see the intentions of the other but before I have distinguished myself ... Reasons ... With the language of love, I am not weird or crazy... My appearance (I love what God created me, walking and running and still standing true, right, no matter how long it takes).....I love myself as I follow justice, practice pure love, speak up the truth, want the best for my self, be compasionand understanding with others. "

110. "Self- love is hard to achieve if not desirable - no plan - no action - faith – no courage to start - incapable to start - fears that may fail- where laziness exist- there are no justice towards self and others - there is a desire for quick things to achieve – purpose pointed to money only – friends are number one- no knowledge of pure love. .. "

111. "The self-love is the bridge I had to cross in order to meet my true powerful self .....you can do it ....if you want to meet your true self that helps you to feel and be happy here and now while you have a clear vision where you heading "

22

"Holistic Spiritual Approach
on Magical Module"

VJOLLCA SADIKU
Co- Founder & Director
Magical Coaching

# 111

## Questions to
## Self Discovery Journey

# 111 Questions to Self Discovery Journey

1) How can we achieve self-love?

2) What does self-love mean?

3) Why do we need self-love?

4) Why are we humans never happy unless we have self-love?

5) Why does our body need love?

6) Why do we crave love…why do we need others to love us?

7) What are the various perspectives such as religion?

8) Is this life a test, that requires us to cleanse ourselves?

9) What is a soul?

10) Does 'Soul' exist?

11) Is there only one religion?

12) If yes, then why are there so many religions?

13) If no, what is the purpose of there being so many religions?

14) Does it matter how many religions there are?

15) What does science say about the vital aspect of love?

16) How do various religions explain serious life threatening diseases?

17) What is a spiritual path?

18) How can you find out who you are and why is important to know the real you?

19) Who is the real you?

20) Why do we die and what is the meaning of this life?

21) Are we meant to suffer or enjoy life?

22) Why do we suffer?

23) How important is self-love to get the answer to all those questions I mentioned?

24) Can self-love bring peace and love, and how that can happen?

25) What respect means to you?

26) What is what is the concept of word "love" for you?

27) What is the difference between passionate love and love?

28) Do you think babies have love within?

29) Do you remember your childhood feeling loved….give example.

30) Where you are now in your state of energy?

31) Where you want to be and how you will get where you like to be?

32) What you're going to do about being where you are and going where you want to be...?

33) How you can be happy exactly where you are and appreciate what you already have …?

34) What you need to change in order to notice the good things that surround you at that moment?

35) How are you going to blend with life?

36) How are you going to manage your inner happiness and outside world balance?

37) How do you understand with balance?

38) How do others affect your situation?

39) How does the length of the journey affect your fulfillment of the purpose here and now?

40) Do we choose our thoughts?

41) How can we choose our thoughts?

42) Do we organize our thoughts?

43) How can we manage and observe our thoughts?

44) Exercise, at this time of your life, which thoughts are you swimming in?

45) Who you are now from point of your thoughts?

46) Who you want to be?

47) How you want your life to be?

48) What do you need to make it happen the life you want?

49) What is the meaning of passionate love for you?

50) How would you like your partner to be? And are you like that? If yes you are ready to meet someone like that if you are not then you need to work with yourself!!!?

51) Can you live alone? Why not? Or why yes?

52) But are you happy if you are with the wrong person?

53) What do you need to do to find the right person for you?

54) What does inspiration mean to you?

55) Think about how inspiration helps your day to day life

56) Think about who does inspire you and why/how?

57) Connect with nature what this mean?

58) Does nature help you focus and concentrate?

59) Does nature allow you to feel inspired?

60) Connect with babies what does it mean and feel?

61) Do babies inspire you and how/why?

62) Care about your needs…how do you do it and how would you like to do it?

63) Why is it important to have inspiration in daily life?

64) What examples of inspiration can you think of?

65) What inspires you daily and what do you get from it?

66) What does Commitment mean to you?

67) What examples of your commitment are you willing to share?

68) How is this example of commitment something other people can learn from?

69) How can we feed love?

70) How to practice spreading love even in dark moments?

71) What is the difference between soul-love and human-love?

72) Are there three main rules according to the life/creator?:

- Treat others as you would like to be treated.

- Love yourself as you would like to be loved.

- Give 100% in everything that you choose.

73)  Are those 3 rules, all that is required of humans to accomplish in this life? How do you explain the way that these can be applied by a person, born in a family amongst members, who do not comply with those rules?

74)  For someone to follow the path that makes them happy, do they firstly have to let go of those who are not happy with themselves, or are becoming obstacles for your journey and will not allow you to achieve your dreams? Even if this encompasses their own family? What is the reason for this?

75)  What is the soul? Where is it located anatomically in humans and what is the role of the soul in this life? Why...

76)  Can a person live and be guided by their soul? How can this be achieved?

77)  Does a bad soul exist? The reason why…

78)  Are the mind, heart and body human utensils, which serve the soul so that the person is faithful or fulfilled? Why...

79)  What does it mean to believe in God and how can this be demonstrated by 3 rules or examples?

80)  Do you suppose that children are like angels and innocent? Why? How is their suffering explained in God's language and why?

81) Are there two kinds of death: A prewritten one and another that depends on our Actions? If so, how is the child's death explained?

82) Can a human-being be filled with love, which comes exclusively from the source within themselves? And from the moment they become aware of that love, they do not feel suffering because they are know their purpose and are fulfilled?

83) What do you think is the love within? And why do you think that way?

84) Why we are born?

85) Why we die?

86) Who control the world?

87) Who has created the world?

88) What is the reason for creating the world and what is our role on it?

89) How can we create a better world ?!!!!

90) Tell me how you describe your self?

91) How others will describe you?

91) How others will describe you?

92) How would you like to be described if you had a magic wound?

93) Can you tell me those three characters you described how can be one? If cant be one why?

94) How can we make it to be one? Or do we need too? Or what should you do with that person that has answered those questions?

95) How to make people to love themselves, others and life ?

96) How can we make people believe that happiness is here and now in whatever we choose to do? And is not in the material world......

97) How can someone who eats only once a day and don't have house to sleep can be happy and love themselves and life here and now?

98) How the child who is with bad parents can still love themselves and life?

99) How can we enjoy working on what we want to achieve?

100)     How an adult can be a child ....
as children are happy most of the times .....
but using the adults power?

101) What advice you give to adults to be happy here and now and achieve their dreams.....?

102) What are your unexplained experiences so far and how would you explain them?

103) What is intuition? Give few examples when intuition was speaking to you?

104) What is most important value in life for you?

105) What do you love about you, life and the world?

106) What does it mean to believe in yourself?

107) How can we discipline ourselves to take the journey to achieving self belief? (An exercise with small steps which leads from the place the individual is currently at to the place they want to be in self love...

108) How important is pure love?

109) 1 to 10 in scales how much you love yourself?

110) What would you do to help the loved ones to be happy here and now?

111) What is the permanent happiness here and now all the times? If can be achieved what does it mean?

"Holistic Spiritual Approach
on Magical Module"

VJOLLCA SADIKU
Co- Founder & Director
Magical Coaching

# Introduction to
## Magical Module Programmes

**What each program is about and why I have categorise it in that way ….**

**Short explanation of each programme of MM** what they bring and what is their purpose and how that can be delivered.

# 1- Explanation of main course: Holistic Spiritual Approach on Magical Module Course….. (HSAOMMC)

This course is to help you gain deep understanding of peace and love here and now for yourself and become qualified to help others achieve the peace and love here and now. Create balance in their lives. Being a holistic spiritual approach based on Magical Module is a very rewarding and lucrative career. You will be able to build your own business, enabling you to create your own schedule, be your own boss, have more freedom and most importantly help others achieve their dreams! And contribute to creating a peaceful and loving world.

This course will be achieved between one year up to three years depending on the individual level of growth.

## 2- Coaching programme

is based on coaching qualifications and principles…completely different from the other programmes in this book. Each life coach has their unique way of delivering their training. My way is to start with deep questions in order to shake your balance completely so you can be able to observe your self from different point of view and then work on the topic you choose to work. The programme is designed for ages *11 years old up to 65 plus*……because everyone needs some help to get into the right path of feeling in peace and love here and now while they enjoy the journey of life. Also to know how to share the love with others around us and to be fully in moment.

35

# 3- Mentoring Programme

Is to give you deep swim into the past in order to heal yourself from any blockage or pain that is stopping you to enjoy the present moment and have no limitation to your future vision. Then will bring to the present to explore the Magical Module (MM) stages and take you to the future in order to understand yourself, others and life. By understanding "you" will know the importance of self-love and work to gain your self-love of MM.....You will learn to be guided by your true self and gain your ability to listen to your intuition anytime you need guidance when you are stuck or confused.

The time scale is minimum three months for each topic which in total will be one year to three years and the age group is 16 until 65 plus........it does cover any issues as long as the individual is not in medication........if it is in medication may interfere with outcome this programme aims to achieve.....because medication interferes with self-healing. Definitely you will get great results more then what you aimed for but not what the programmes aim....

Contracts have to be designed based on the, institution, individual or groups needs and requirements.

# 4-Focus Therapy on one Problem Presented

The forty eight (48) ingredients of knowing if you are doing your best:
Time scale is three months

# 5: Youth program 16 to 18...or 25 ..

This programme is introduction to MM coaching programme or Mentoring programme and time scale is one month. The reason I left it free to flow by young person is because ......I feel their confusion, fear, desperation to feel loved, scared of the future, hurt when they think of the people they love.....etc....etc .....and I know they will feel it each step of MM with their passion, imagination, essence of love, and lots of different dreams including amazing courage and inspiration. They are our future and we have to support them to be in the path they dream of being.

## 6-Fostering HSAOMM Program /Foster Carer and Child

….Time scale for this programme may take between one year and three years to achieve the outcome of HSAOMMP.

(can I put in top of each page the name "Holistic Spiritual Approach of Magical Module Programme")

This programme is just summery of structure of the programme as it has to be designed and personalised based on individual cases…..as each case is unique. For more details you can look the depth content of holistic spiritual approach of magical module programme to have understanding of the purpose the programme have.

## 7- Local Authority / All Professionals Holistic Spiritual Approach of Magical Module Program …..."Self-love"

(Time scale can be between one months to three months or just full one day training just for introduction…..but for training to work need one year to three year time scale depending on the progress and level of requirement).

The purpose of programmes are to help the world become a place of love and peace where people can enjoy life, BE FULLY HAPPY HERE AND NOW AND WORK TOWARDS THEIR AIMS AND GOALS WITH OUT HURTING OTHERS. The solution is gaining self-love…..self discovery through practising purity ….be who they meant to be ….Be happy within 100%

*This programme will be mainly to introduce to all professionals how important is self-love, what it is self-love and how can it be achieved….. Therefore will be just on paragraph for few different professions to explain why they role will make huge difference to contributing to creating and building world of peace and love if they work to gain self-love in order to be happy all the times here and now …...so then they will be able to apply pure love practice into their role of work and so on ……Become the change the world need in order to be a place of love and harmony of joy.*

The main problems that need attention from the professionals are below: That's why I created a self-love programme for professionals because if they have not yet gained self-love …..they will not be able to help others gain or guide towards gaining self-love…..Self-love is solution to all those concerns below

Teenagers (bulling, gang, coping with pear pressure, )

Criminals in prison…to help them discover their true potential and turn their life around

Children in care to explore the options and chose the right path

Homeless …helping them to get up and support them to get on their feet

People with serious illness….help them to accept what is going on and explore the options how to enjoy the present and plan for tomorrow

People with different mental issues  ….help them heal through self love to understand their mind and heart…

People who find it hard to commit to relationships….and how to find the right one……which they are experiencing depression and other issues

Professionals to gain their self-love in order to do their job properly into higher standards

Business owners to help them gain their self love in order to achieve their full potential, enjoy the present and have a detailed plan of what they want to achieve …..in order to have their business flowing and have more then enough time to enjoy life

Parents to improve their relationship with their children and be content with their life

Couples to improve their relationships and work towards true love…

Old age to overcome their loneliness

Lots more problems are that the world experiences ……

## What are my reasons of creating those programmes in the way I have created…

Each programme is just a power points to what I will be talking about …..exercises may be provided in few programmes as general example but I like to focus on the bullet points as the exercise and the way of explanation flow will be personalised based on the individual, group , organisation, institution, or on the topic is presented at the moment. Magical Module is just the general structure to help others create their own way of creation as long as the base is based on Magical Module principles and values. I do believe everyone is unique and have ability to use their creativity…..just have to be the believe and want towards peace and love here and now…

In this course you will learn to identify the difference between yourself and true self that you are created, along with how to discern the difference in others as well, which will help communication. You'll learn what triggers you to react, and get to the root of why you feel the anger, fear, anxiety, and other emotions that are holding you back. We will also explore the positive aspects your true self brings to the party that is you (soul, mind, heart, body). You'll develop skills to bridge your communication with higher energy, your higher self, others and life. Leading to a more balanced way of living in the world that fills your life with joy, laughter, fun, success, and healthy relationships.

39

What are some of the benefits Holistic Spiritual Approach Magical Module programs will bring..... Because are lots more to be designed as is applied and each achievement is unique based on the work commitment is provided by you.

Can help homeless people in three months to get back on their own feet.....

Can empower troubled children age 11 to 25 to act on their potential and gain self-love....

Can encourage parents to gain self-love...

Can encourage couple's to work towards true love.....

Can encourage parent to learn babies language......the language of love...

Can help criminals to turn their life around towards gaining self-love......

Can educate professionals to gain self-love in order to be able to do the job role properly...

Build a bridge for children in care in order their wellbeing to blossom and to achieve their potential.....to show them that the life is amazing and all challenges are just to help the grow to the person they meant to be....

What are some of the benefits Holistic Spiritual Approach Magical Module programs will bring.....
Because are lots more to be designed as is applied and each achievement is unique based on the work commitment is provided by you.

Help foster carers to keep the balance of that bridge and enjoy what they do ....

Can contribute to creating a world of peace and love

Love yourself and others, find out who you are, create your own life, be yourself

Help you find compassion and self-love for yourself and for others in all areas of your life

Help you understand unhealthy patterns you have in your life so that you can break them

Help you understand and connect with people on a deeper level

Can contribute to understanding different stages of children in order to fulfil their potential and adults to learn to provide the right guidance for children.... Children by nature are to grow and blossom

- To heal wounds, especially the deep-rooted wounds we aren't consciously aware of, we must explore all the different parts of who we are, from inception to now. By doing that, we truly learn to nurture, love, heal, and grow within ourselves and with others. By finally acknowledging and healing that wound, we discover that buried part of us we know is there, yet can never seem to get to. Not understanding all of who we are prevents us from living in what we know as our fullest potential.

41

You'll receive, over the course of one year to three years different programmes designed personalised to your needs and followed up with homework and clear guidance of what you need in further to achieve your permanent happiness here and now and have clear plan for tomorrow vision.

Each time you commit to working with Magical Module guidance is full in-depth work that will allow you to work on the different parts of you…. to bring healing and changes in your life you have been seeking. Each stages of Magical Module (MM) include tools for you to grow and became closer to who you desire to be….who you meant to be …..and fully happy within here and now …..reflection of your own happiness can shine through you into outside world in whatever you choose to do….

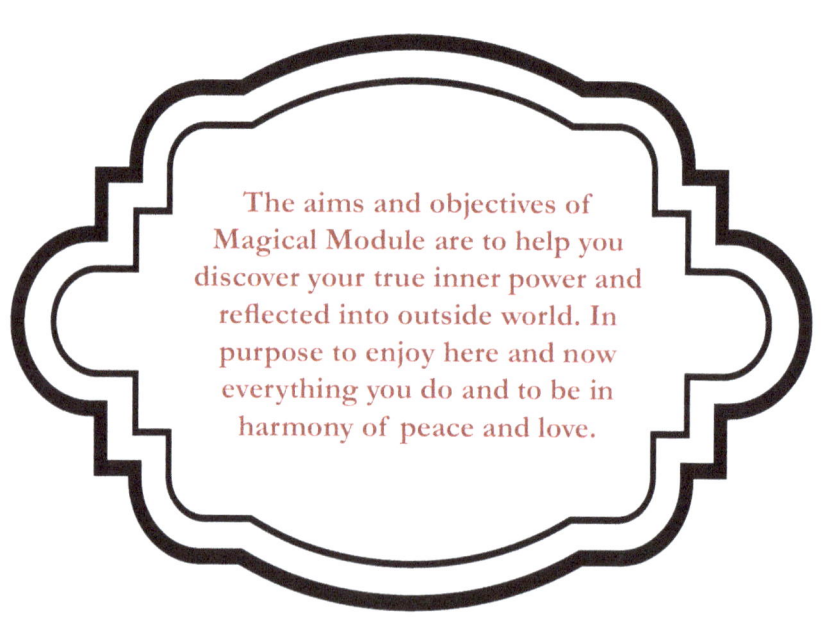

The aims and objectives of Magical Module are to help you discover your true inner power and reflected into outside world. In purpose to enjoy here and now everything you do and to be in harmony of peace and love.

"Self discovery journey is link to your life path purpose.....and it will be reviewed with clear outlook in the time between death and rebirth....."

Self-discovery have few stages:

To make yourself happy here and now with everything you choose to do .....as we do have choice how to react to outside world ....

Learning how to maintain that contentment achieved on stage one .....

Exploring in more depth your life purpose .....how to make use of yourself better? How to contribute to loved ones around you? .....what are your abilities?....explore your gifts ....

Get our self out there and test your abilities....test what you decided to do from stage three ....

Retreat yourself in more deep self discovery and get all in .......be one with universe and have a deep chat where you want to go ....what is your next step ....evaluate your self discovery and life path.....choose what makes you happy here and now.........as you continue fulfilling your life purpose....

Don't know yet as I have not reached it yet ....but I know it is stage six and stage seven......or could be up to stage eleven.....

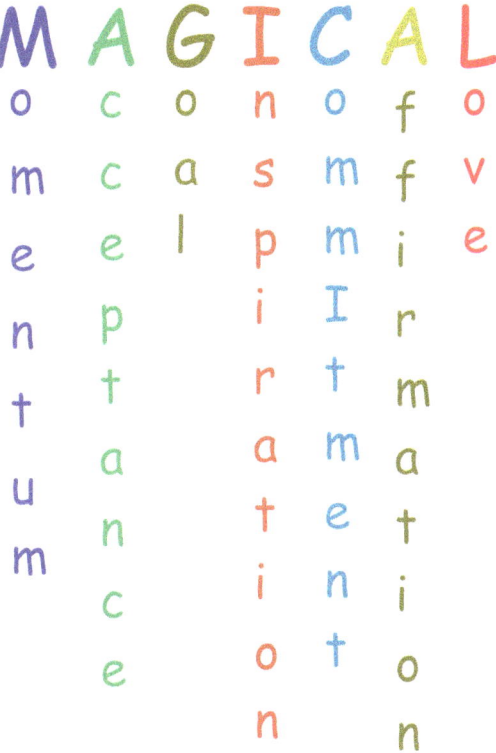

**M A G I C A L**

| M | A | G | I | C | A | L |
|---|---|---|---|---|---|---|
| o | c | o | n | o | f | o |
| m | c | a | s | m | f | v |
| e | e | l | p | m | i | e |
| n | p |   | i | I | r |   |
| t | t |   | r | t | m |   |
| u | a |   | a | m | a |   |
| m | n |   | t | e | t |   |
|   | c |   | i | n | i |   |
|   | e |   | o | t | o |   |
|   |   |   | n |   | n |   |

*100% those achievement below can be achieved if you follow the guidance of MM. (This achievement applies only for people who are healthy physically and are not in any medication because for those who are in medication will take twice longer or more).*

## ⚡First part of the work is:

First three months will achieve to introduce your self to whole new window of life: Discovering who you are …30 days, Connecting with intuition …90 days, How to find your true wishes/desires, What you want to do with your life, Build your

Knowing **your** whole you, **soul,** body, heart **and** mind.

confidence in 30 to 90 days, Having a clear plan of what you like to change, knowledge of how to practice self-love automatically, Learn how to create stepping stones to get where you want to be, How to self guide yourself, How to be in the moment and enjoy it, to Stop reflect/evaluate your life/steps/plan, How to love everything you do, Feed yourself with love energy, Enjoy your magical life you have it as you continue the work of MM to the second part of the work.

## ⚡ Second part of the work is:

this part of work
also takes three months.

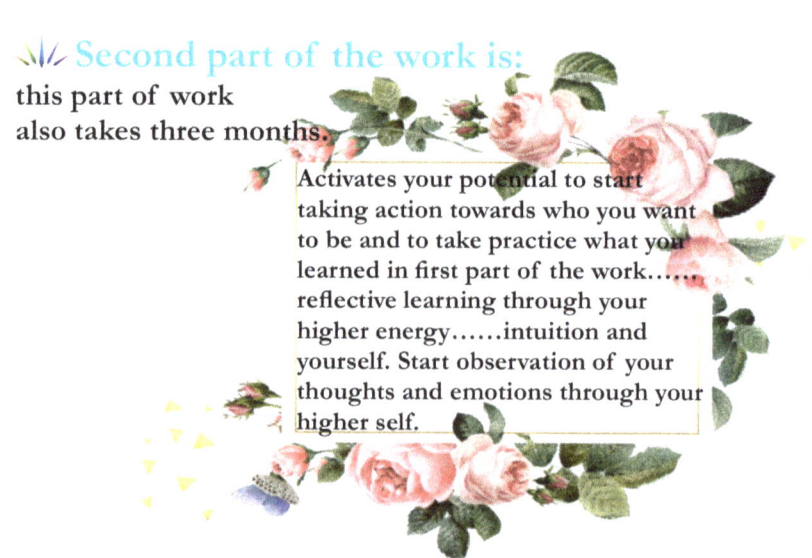

Activates your potential to start taking action towards who you want to be and to take practice what you learned in first part of the work…… reflective learning through your higher energy……intuition and yourself. Start observation of your thoughts and emotions through your higher self.

## 🌿 Third part of the work is: Also this part will take three months to six months.

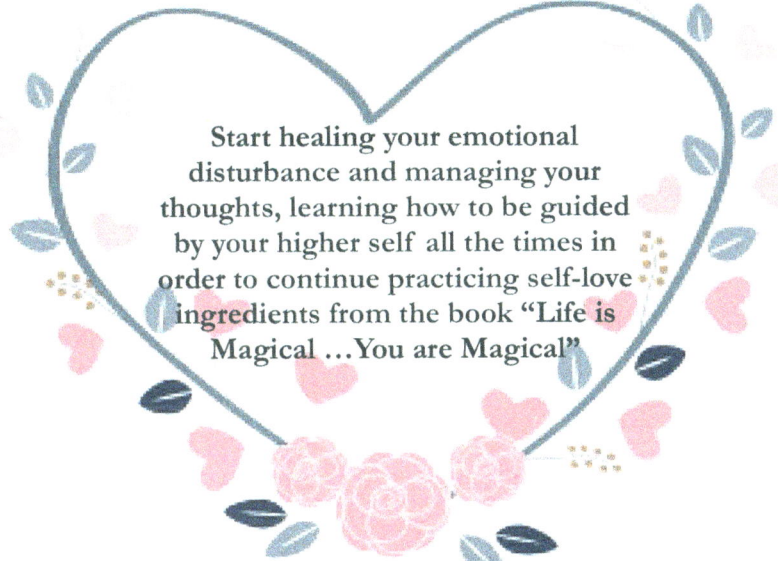

Start healing your emotional disturbance and managing your thoughts, learning how to be guided by your higher self all the times in order to continue practicing self-love ingredients from the book "Life is Magical …You are Magical"

Rules of being happy here and now...and part of practice in this stage are:
1- treating yourself right
2- not hurting anyone
3- Working hard for what you want to achieve

The right education need to be on education system to teach people how to be happy.....
Self-love ingredients are the bridge to being happy, content, in harmony here and now with anything you decide to do.....is the bridge to your higher self.
How to be happy means being fulfilled here and now and can be achieved by practising purity that lead to pure self-love (to know your true self and your real purpose on this life....and then you are able to hear and believe on Creator )....
Who can achieve pure self-love can never hurt others and is happy here and now while they know where they want to be and how to get there ..
"We should not be scared of death or what others do to us because our light still will be on .....

47

we should be scared of doing wrong to ourselves and others because that will make us be in dark ........being in light means you are happy exactly where you are and you have clear plan for future....also you never hurt yourself or others .......being in dark means it does not matter how good your reality is ...you still not satisfied and feel that emptiness inside you ...which lead to doing wrong to yourself and others "

Which is to help being guided by the soul (our pure true self that never dies) and listening to intuition (the voice of creator)...in order to feed the brain and heart only with pure healthy thoughts .....this can be achieved by gain self-love....

Who has gained self-love is fulfilled exactly where they are and how they are ....feel in peace and loved...also have detailed plan how to get what they want ...

You'll also learn how to tune the two most powerful neural networks in your body for super-learning, deep intuitive wisdom, and self-healing.
Because all the psychological theories are to explain the humans behaviours and very little on explaining solutions to a happy life ...fulfilled, peaceful and filled with lots of love .....
My theory is based on the cause of problems and solutions with time scale....
Because we are product of pure love and practising daily what we are made off ......will help us to be happy, fulfilled, peaceful and off feeling loved here and now .........

The causes of the problems are not practising what we are made .off....

If the individual have not achieved the self-love ....it means they are in a problem zone ....in a journey of healing and growth but with out right guidance and it keeps going in circle of painful emotional experiences.

## ⋏⎮⎰ Part four of the MM work: This is about keeping the balance of what you have learned so far and create your own tools how to continue keeping the harmony of balance and exploring options how to contribute to the world.

You are ready to move through any obstacles that come your way, with a courageous and joyous heart. There is always a solution. There is always a great way forward. Sometimes our internal struggle and resistance to the challenges we face, very much further complicate things, yet, may you always be a soul who remains light and full of solutions and have sharpened your conversations with your intuition.

You have to allows remember: For a joyful life here and now we only have to connect with our deepest core .....which is pure love (soul) and guide our life in pure love guidance......which is the soul and intuition....

When you achieve that ....
You are able to understand other's and life and give the right support to who you want to support or contribute into the world .....
Qualifications can not teach you how to be you .....they only can give you directions....and signs but if you don't see it as direction and signs and allow them to guide your life journey.....you are living someone's life and completely ignoring yourself ..........which lead to not doing with pure love the job you are doing ....and also making you living unfulfilled life.

What happens when those benefits are not achieved as promised?......
I am very sure it can't happen because I will make sure you are following the guidance of MM and if you are not following then we have to pause our work until you are ready to continue.... All will be in contract clear and straightforward structure of MM. Remember the self help program is free for you to practice it on your own and will be free few emails for free to help you on your self help journey. ......self-help journey can be achieved the aims of MM between one year to 5 years depending on the level of your growth and your commitment on the work you do on MM.

"Holistic Spiritual Approach on Magical Module"

VJOLLCA SADIKU
Co- Founder & Director
Magical Coaching

# Holistic Spiritual Approach of Magical Module Course:

# 15 Stages

# Holistic Spiritual Approach
## of Magical Module Course:

To help you to be happy, fulfilled, in peace and loved here and now: 15th stages of self-love program from age 7 years old and up to 65 years old plus....also to be qualified to provide training for others if you wish.....tests will be provided during the course.

# Stage 1

Who are we?

Introduction to us, others and the world ....life ...

We are created to be happy, fulfilled here and now, in peace and feeling loved. Why? Because we meant to create an amazing world ....paradise where love is shared and everything is done from base of pure love. What is pure love? Pure love is combination of the energy of babies, abilities of children and the power of adult.

51

**Power point 1:** (Through the exercises designed based on the individual needs will help them to understand the three points below in order to know how powerful they are).

### 1. The energy of the babies

*The energy of babies is pure and the reason is pure is because we are created from purity in order to come to this life with free will and free choice to create our life journey. (In more details will be explained in momentum stage).*

### 2. Abilities of children

*Abilities of children are unlimited; they have great creativity and vision to do so much. Children are great guidance for adults and they come up with solution for everything because their intelligence is based on energy of babies'. (This point can be explained in depth in stage of acceptance, affirmation and inspiration)*

### 3. Power of adult

*Power of adult is huge because they have the power of choice and they are the one who can make final decision. (This point can be explained in depth through goal, commitment and love stage).*

People have to learn to focus on loving vibrations of babies, rather than hate vibrations of adults, or lower vibrations of mind and heart, if you are focusing on what people have done to you, or what they did and focusing on the negatives that is low vibrations, as long as you give those things credence you are allowing yourself to feed into it, and you create the very things you are trying to avoid. People and things can only be given as much power as you allow because you are a master of your own life by using the adult's power. The power of making decisions on how you will react to outside world and your inner world.

If you shift your focus on what you can do based on those three points I mentioned and concentrate on what others are doing just as lessen or to stimulate your creativity of your power, you will shift the power and will be operating from higher vibration. In love and divine light.

---

*Power point 2:* Baby's language is the language of love and it starts from energy stage. (This power point is to help you introduce to abilities of communication skills we have been given).

**The language of love is the language of babies that it continues on the stages below:**

1.Language of energy

2. Language of body language

 # Language of energy

I have been learning about energy language since I was 7 years old as I asked to communicate with the energy we are created and who is in charge of creating us. (My life journey have been explained in my first book "A Magical Life" where is explained in details how I have applied Magical Module to create my Magical life journey.) How?

Because I refused to be part of the energy I was surrounded as explained in my first book "A Magical Life", And in second book "Life is Magical …You are Magical" I backed it up with the research I did based on what others have said, 50 questioners with 11 open questions, social media discussion, on feedback from my first book and how Magical Module is applied to 30 clients. In my second book is explained and demonstrated in details my work through different levels of communication with others.

Since age of 7 years old I only followed the message from intuition "love yourself and love life" .....and that given me skills how to maintain practising purity.....and by practising purity you master your energy level of communication.....

Of course I forgot to keep remembering what happened when I was 7 years old as I grown up ....specially when my dream of falling in love and living happy after did not happen....that unbalanced my energy and took me in a journey of discovery how to keep loving myself and life when I did not have the right partner on my side ......

Until age 36 years old I was angry with my family because they did not give me the freedom to meet the right one....also the search for the right one was not going well......

.

then I had to stop searching for the right partner but I started to gain self-love...... I said to myself " are you thick, are you stupid, why are you waiting for someone to love you in order to be happy....why? If you can't love yourself how someone can love you ?.....
You need to start loving yourself and feel fulfilled here and now"
......
It took me one year to work on my energy....to clean it and master it ...

Which mean I am a master of my energy ........and worked on purity.
And I am master of meditation forms as it took me one year to practice and develop different meditation in order to travel back on my past and in my future in order to master my energy.....to serve me the way I wanted to serve me ....me is my soul....my spiritual being part of the Creator.....universe....
When I was 36 years old it was 2012 ....and in 2013 I was wake spiritually....time to explore.......
In 2013 up to 2017 as I was growing and enjoying feeling happy here and now....I managed to publish my first book....then was an upgrade in my spiritual journey as I started to master listening and follow intuition.....
Intuition (the voice of Creator) was guiding me as if took me to a journey of my second book .....''Life is Magical...You are Magical " ....that the skills I had learned I applied in others and created a self-help program in chapter three where you can achieve to master your energy....to be guided by the soul and intuition .....Exactly what I had done on myself..... the program is for free to read it on the link below:
http://www.holisticmagicalapproach.com/post-title932d3106

I realised that I have been working through the language of energy, work in whole themselves and learn how to use the energy in their favour in order to be happy here and now and have clear plan about where they are heading..... our energy is very powerful and that's what healing happens when I work with clients....

The outcome of Magical Module is guaranty 100%....if you want to test Magical Module.....the self-help program in chapter three of the book "Life is Magical..You are Magical" that is for free on the link above .....you are welcome....and you will have 5 free emails to contact me through the whole year of the work you will do in Magical Module....and if it is need it ...you can have a whole day with me doing intense work after you have finished practising chapter three....the self-help program....

Then you can tested if it works or not .....as I know 100% it will work.....

### Now in my understanding of energy is:

Soul and spirit means the same thing to me ....is our spiritual being ....pure energy

Intuition is the voice of Creator....universe....same thing ....creator and universe is one ....or universe is the house of creator and that's why I feel the same energy from both ....the only difference is that intuition is 100% the voice of Creator and is firm voice....the universe is like a love energy and guides me through flow and visualization....helps me to travel and see things that I need to see and learn ....is like holding my hand...

The energy can be considered as a 'mirror' that reveals our present mental, emotional, physical and spiritual state. ....and is around us like a meter circle around us.....

Through this programme you will learn how to master and use the language of energy, how to recharge it , how to work on healing skills of being in others energy, how to read the energy, how to protect your self from others, how to decide when to open your energy circle and how to keep it close in order not to absorb the others energy with out need........and that's what I work very well with my client's....

Self-help Magical module can help you to do the same ..and is free to practice it on the link I provide it above .....as self help or I can teach you through this programme.

The language of the energy is very important to practice it in order to be in the right path to your happiness journey.

Our soul and intuition is pure... language of the babies energy

Spiritual being

Soul and spirit means the same thing to me .... is our spiritual being .... pure energy ...

Pure energy

universe....same thing ....creator and universe is one .... and universe is the house of creator or universe is the house of creator

Universe

Intuition is the voice of Creator

Intuition

The energy can be considered as a 'mirror' that reveals our present mental, emotional, physical and spiritual state ... and is around us like a meter circle around us....

Energy

*Now in my understanding of energy is:*

"The path of light is like going into darkness with confidence and self believe in yourself and the creator..." ... during this path you will be facing challenges, fall down, get hurt, rushing, wanting to turn back/give up, doubting yourself and the creator because you do not see the light but simply walk in darkness with confidence on yourself and creator. You will bang your head by the wall, , you will scream, you will be afraid, you will ask to see, seek comfort and stop, will have the desire to lie and cheat but ..... the sensation you feel during your journey can not be exchanged with anything else and therefore you continues because everything seems to be adventure and love ......

It takes a lot of discipline with yourself to walk in the enlightened way ... and the language of energy is the main language to learn.

**1. Appreciate what you have**

**2. To understand others and the outside world**

**3. To love yourself and your life without hurting anybody**

**4. Ask for what you need to feel loved within**

**5. To forgive yourself but not to repeat the mistakes**

In order to create good energy you need to do at least the steps below for starter:

**6. To criticize yourself when you notice that you are going in the wrong way or trying to deviate**

**7. Stay in the centre ... at soul energy and intuition**

**8. Ask forgiveness when you are wrong**

**9. Not to oppose the criticism of the other but to discuss it and understanding it..... also to appreciate it**

**10. Appreciate time the other is dedicating to you**

**11. And continue to enjoy the adventure of life journey**

Whatever you intend to create in your life involves generating the same life-giving quality that brings everything into existence. The spirit of anything, the quality that allows it to come into the world of form, is true as a general principle, so why not activate it within you? The power of intention simply awaits your ability to make the connection.

Remember energy creates anything around us and the energy is not pure from everything because is based on the creation of the thoughts human use. That's why I am pointing out only the energy of the babies is pure and that's why I am referring to that, as it is great example.

**Language of body language** is expression of our energy language. In order to understand the body language you have to learn the language of energy first. Children operate from pure energy until they reach age of 25 and than around age 36 we have another sign to remind us to go back and create our life journey based on pure energy language.

How do you enter into the spirit of intention, which is all about feelings expressing life? You can nurture it by your continual on going expectation of the infallible spiritual law of increase being a part of your life. We saw it through our imaginary capacity to see higher vibrations, and we heard it in the voice given to it by spiritual masters throughout the ages. It's everywhere. It wants to express life. It's pure love in action. It's confident. And guess what? You are it, but you've forgotten. You need to simply trust your ability to cheerfully rely upon Spirit to express itself through and for you. Your task is to contemplate the energies of life, love, beauty, and kindness. Every action that's in harmony with this originating principle of intention gives expression to your own power of intention.

The psychologist explains very well the body language of people who are not happy but I am interested to bring you solution to the road of permanent happiness. For that reason I will focus on the road of solution and once you enter the road of solution....road of pure language of energy you will understand the rest of your psychological things including your illness.

**Language of words** is created by the way we have been feeding our mind through our childhoods and our life journey up to now. Our neuroplasticine minds receive the imprints and shapes of the major narratives of our immediate environment. The way our parents spoke and interacted, the way we were treated at school. This then goes into the subconscious pool of thoughts and behaviours and fundamental ideas about life, the world and our relationships. We believe the subconscious ideas as truth or fact so get hoodwinked time and again by them and we forget our language of energy to practice it because we have not been taught by outside environment. Unless healed, those narratives will still play out in adulthood, causing limiting and punishing behaviours.

Our job in adulthood is to cease limiting narratives and gain freedom and spiritual sovereignty through going back to learn the language we have been born with.

One way is to simply notice a narrative coming up and then deliberately deselecting it, breathing through it, letting it go.

What are the self-limiting narratives that come up for you that you used to believe but that now you'd like to give up?

Through the stages of Magical Module you will have clear steps how to shift your way of communication with yourself, others and life from in the right way …..not the way we have learned from outside world.

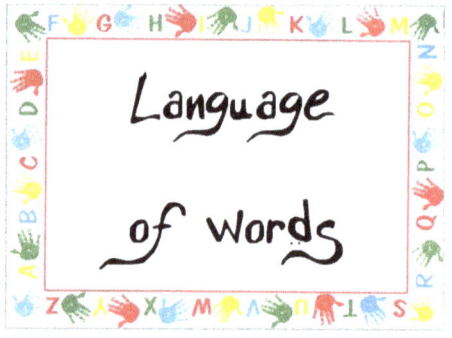

is created by the way we have been feeding our mind through our childhoods and our life journey up to now. Our neuroplasticine minds receive the imprints and shapes of the major narratives of our immediate environment. The way our parents spoke and interacted, the way we were treated at school. taught by outside environment. Unless healed, those narratives will still play out in adulthood, causing limiting and punishing behaviours.

Our job in adulthood is to cease limiting narratives and gain freedom and spiritual sovereignty through going back to learn the language we have been born with.

One way is to simply notice a narrative coming up and then deliberately deselecting it, breathing through it, letting it go.

What are the self-limiting narratives that come up for you that you used to believe but that now you'd like to give up?

Through the stages of Magical Module you will have clear steps how to shift your way of communication with yourself, others and life from in the right way …..not the way we have learned from outside world.

# Communication learned from world is:

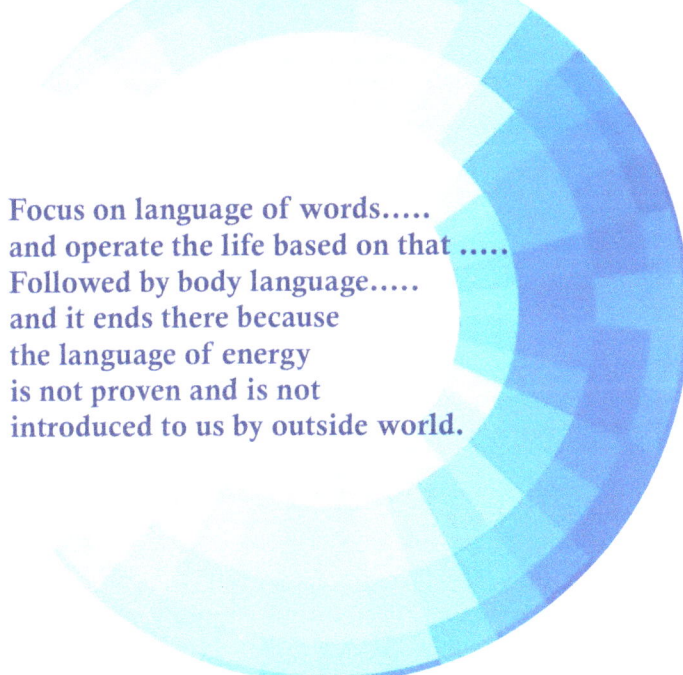

Focus on language of words…..
and operate the life based on that …..
Followed by body language…..
and it ends there because
the language of energy
is not proven and is not
introduced to us by outside world.

# Communication given by creator

Communication given by creator
since we are born  is the energy
language......followed by body
language and then spoken language.

Power point 3: Introduction to understanding our existence,
why we are here and how we and life work ...

**1** Why we are created, what is the purpose of our existence? (The explanation will be in detailed in chapter two of the book "Life is Magical...You are Magical")

**2** Why is important to practice self-love ingredients and how they are link to us, others and life? (Because is the bridge to connect with our true self.......).

**3** What is the role of creator and how we have been operated? (it must be someone who has created us as we do get born and we die also .....also if we pay attention they are lots of things mysterious that can be explained only by tuning into our inner world.....and what is our inner world?)

How to gain self-love (be guided by your soul) ...and sharpen your intuition (the voice of creator) to create the reality you want .....which lead to being fulfilled, in peace and feeling loved exactly where you are and having detailed plan where you heading in future....

This power point will primarily focus on the foundation of its core premise: self-love, which, with the appropriate tools and techniques, is the key to opening the doors to a number of further questions and explore ways to real and permanent contentment.

**Remember:**

No soul does guide anyone to do evil or the wrong things towards themselves or others.......but is the mind and heart feed it from information outside world......
The prove that every soul is pure can be proven in babies............
As we grow we disconnect with the soul and intuition......but who has gained back self-love is connected to their soul.........
To gain self-love....it means you are fulfilled, in peace and feel loved exactly where you are and you have detailed plan how to get what you want for future......
You never hurt anyone or do wrong to anyone......self-love is pure love towards your self, others and life......

*Soul is part of our inner world....*

*part of creator....*

63

# Exercise 1:

| Answers |
| --- |
|  |
|  |
|  |
|  |
|  |
|  |
|  |
|  |
|  |
|  |
|  |

Tell me how you describe your self?

How others will describe you?

How would you like to be described if you had a magic wound?

Can you tell me those three characters you described how can be one?

If cant be one why?

How can we make it to be one?

Or do we need too?

Or what should you do with that person that has answered those questions?

# *Exercise 2:* | Answers

Why we are born?

Why we die?

Who control the world?

Who has created the world ?

What is the reason for creating the world and what is our role on it ?

How can we create a better world ?!!!!

"An individual who does not achieve fulfilment, peace, and feel full of love ....has no ability to understand the life meaning or believe in the creator ....Because the first thing that does if you believes in the creator is to find happiness , fulfilment, peace and living in harmony with love here and now "

One specific problem you are facing at the moment and how we can look at with the attitude we just talked about .....write down your issue....look at minimum three options....write minimum three reasons why has caused it ...give three option how can you prevented.... If was your child in your place what would you suggest to them?

## Discuss/exercise:

-Chapter TWO on the book "Life is Magical...You are Magical" and my experience at age of 7
-Need to ask ...... what are you thinking and where your thinking  is taking you ....
-Create an exercise to help you go in deep thinking .....to connect with your soul....with your pure side ....in order to come up with answers of questions below.

Let's see if we can answer those questions below

| Questions for you | Answers |
|---|---|
| | |

1- Are there three main rules according to the Lord?:
-  Treat others as you would like to be treated.
-  Love yourself as you would like to be loved.
-  Give 100% in everything that you choose.

2- Are those 3 rules, all that is required of humans to accomplish in this life? How do you explain the way that these can be applied by a person, born in a family amongst members, who do not comply with those rules?

3- For someone to follow the path that makes them happy, do they firstly have to let go of those who are not happy with themselves, or are becoming obstacles for your journey and will not allow you to achieve your dreams? Even if this encompasses their own family? What is the reason for this?

# Questions for you | Answers

4- What is the soul? Where is it located anatomically in humans and what is the role of the soul in this life? Why...

5- Can a person live and be guided by their soul? How can this be achieved?

6 -Does a bad soul exist? The reason why…

7- Are the mind, heart and body human utensils, which serve the soul so that the person is faithful or fulfilled? Why...

8- What does it mean to believe in God and how can this be demonstrated by 3 rules or examples?

9- Do you suppose that children are like angels and innocent? Why? How is their suffering explained in God's language and why?

# Questions for you

# Answers

10- Are there two kinds of death: A prewritten one and another that depends on our Actions? If so, how is the child's death explained?

11 - Can a human-being be filled with love, which comes exclusively from the source within themselves? And from the moment they become aware of that love, they do not feel suffering because they are know their purpose and are fulfilled? What do you think is the love within? And why do you think that way?

*And discuss the answers of others including their answer!!!*

# Stage 2

# Exercise one to understand the whole you /voices

## How to recognise the inner voices....

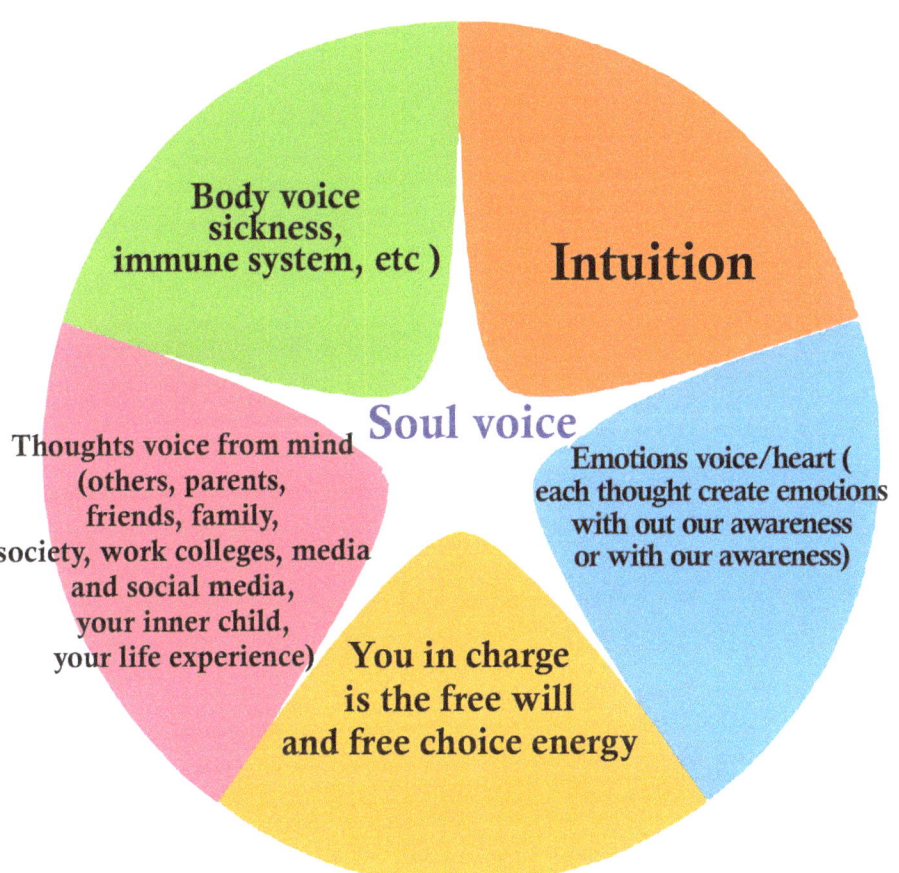

Body voice sickness, immune system, etc )

Intuition

Soul voice

Thoughts voice from mind (others, parents, friends, family, society, work colleges, media and social media, your inner child, your life experience)

Emotions voice/heart ( each thought create emotions with out our awareness or with our awareness)

You in charge is the free will and free choice energy

Create a map or boxes on your preference to put what each inner voice is telling you

# Exercise two

On understanding your unexplained experiences. ...because in order to be clear with yourself and to have clear vision of what you want and need...... is to know the meaning of what is happening to you and how you are reacting the way you are reacting.

Answers

There are two ways of doing this exercise:

1-Write down all unexplained exercises plus your free thoughts of the moment

2-Give your explanation pretending you are advising someone else who has experience what you have experience.....or your younger self under age of 7 can tell you what they think.

# Exercise

# Answers

To get in touch with yourself ….

Say what yourself in different ages will tell you about the way you are living your life?

Example:

My 7 year old I would say ..."keep going ..don't give up ..I am proud of you "
My 10 year old self " I am so happy for you that you are so happy and can see through things and people clear "
To my self now "just be the way you are ....let others think you are crazy but never give up on your vision.....keep going through love and joy "

Need to be explained some roles and words to be educated for a happy life and where we get a free spirit in the harmony of the beauty of life ...... lets see where we got the definition of each from where and what we think should be?

Exercise

# Life Codes:

❋ Responsibility _____

❋ Love _____

❋ Ability _____

❋ Purity _____

❋ Others _____

❋ Love for others _____

❋ Independence _____

❋ Communication _____

❋ Decisions _____

❋ Enjoying the
moment _____

❋ Quietness _____

❋ Relaxation _____

Need to be explained some roles and words to be educated for a happy life and where we get a free spirit in the harmony of the beauty of life …… lets see where we got the definition of each from where and what we think should be?

Exercise

# Life Codes:

🌸 The conversation with high energy, intuition and soul

🌸 Communicating with the other telepathically

🌸 Respect

🌸 Dedication towards work

🌸 Desires

🌸 Search

🌸 Helper of Self, the soul and intuition

🌸 Contribution

Need to be explained some roles and words to be educated for a happy life and where we get a free spirit in the harmony of the beauty of life ...... lets see where we got the definition of each from where and what we think should be?

Exercise

# Life Codes:

* Understanding yourself

_____

* Understanding others

_____

* To love yourself and the other kindness and justice

_____

* Discussion

_____

* Critics

_____

* Contradiction

_____

* Different thoughts

_____

* Fact and opinion

_____

* Happiness

_____

Need to be explained some roles and words to be educated for a happy life and where we get a free spirit in the harmony of the beauty of life ...... lets see where we got the definition of each from where and what we think should be?

Exercise

# Life Codes:

✳ Freedom options and choices _____

✳ How it serves _____

✳ Healthy courage _____

✳ Protection _____

✳ Use and creation of energy _____

✳ Education _____

✳ Source of wisdom _____

More then you shine …..more challenges you will have because the darkness will be shaken…..and your road has to be clear….new doors will be keep opening….

Key thing to get into the wrong path is loneliness….. is the huge problem….it creates emptiness and we have not been educated to keep feeding it with pure self-love but with achieving things ……and this has to change in order for a peaceful and loving world…..and to understand those key words of life operating …..instead of repressing things we suppose to let free our thoughts and feelings…..in order to understand them and come to conclusion of what we want to do with ourselves and life journey we are on.

Emptiness    Running    Search    Material things and love from others

Confusion

Disappointment

# Loneliness…. repressed

This brings a life with complaints and turbulence

Hurt

Again continues in the same circle    Emptiness    Discomfort    Suffering

Emptiness    Self-talk    Notes    Clarifications
of thoughts

# Free
# Loneliness....

Clarification of
feelings

When you feel it again ...you
start from the beginning this
technique .... it brings peace,
harmony and love ....

And
examining
everything

Peace of
mind by
where it
comes
that
emptiness

Action    Notes

Organization    Planning    Ending    Discussion

Harmony    Desire    Understanding    Meaning

# To want

Beyond
the
present

Harmony
Peace

Options

Love    Sustainability

Space
Live    Commitments

Decision    Faith

imagine like you
have it.
…visualise and
wanted again

What you
have to do to
accomplish it

Why do you
deserve it

Confidence

Dream   Vision Discussion   Realistic   Decision   Plan

# To dream

Action

Hold strong after faith

Confidence

Hug
self - love

Respect freedom
of life

Self believe

Love
the fear

Desire

Enjoy the air ......

Courage

Feeling
down

Plan

Analyse the
process and
outcome

Suspicion

Start again

Doubt

Strengthen
confidence
and self
believe

Discussion

Return to the
belief of the
faith and
vision

81

# How to connect with your soul:

Dedicate some time everyday to yourself. Have deep and insightful conversations as you discover your inner peace. You will discover your inner child, whose dreams have no limit and whose imagination is free to explore and sail. You'll fly without even realising, you'll find peace and love and you'll suddenly find the courage to do anything you put your mind to. Once you've discovered the courage inside you, hold onto that feeling and keep practicing that exercise for as long as you need. The second step follows after this. (but the ingredients must only be goodness in every flow or to create imagination).

Begin working with your mind. You can do this by yourself in silence having felt that you've learned from step one, where your soul observes the mind with love and successfully organises your thoughts  through compassion. You must let go of the thoughts that don't serve your pure love, justice and inner peace and alternatively construct thoughts which reflect the reality you desire. This is a process in itself because every new thought should be accompanied by a detailed plan of what you will do and how you will do it. With practice you'll be able to create only thoughts, which serve your soul. The initial feeling at the first step, which is associated with justice, kindness and love brings satisfaction as it gives you a hint of where you are and where you want to be.

At this stage you must turn your attention to your heart, which requires special care as it is sensitive and delicate. The heart tends to contradict the thoughts but at the same time each though creates a feeling. If your thoughts are not filled with love, which protect you from the unjust actions of other individuals, then they create feelings of hurt and pain. Thus, this process takes longer than  that of the mind and is far more difficult as there will be pain, tears, a feeling of the loss of love. However, this pain can be healed through the love of the soul. This process continues until all the hurtful feelings are healed by the care of the soul ... and produces only feelings of love.

Now we must turn to the body and follow the process relating to the body. Exploring any physical pain, exploring how connected you are with your body, exploring the food the body needs and what which kind of food do  you give and why, thinking for long term to have a healthy body, thinking the ways your body feeds through love (sleep, free of stress, exercise, relaxed, how do you give love).

By this step we bring together all the previous steps, which combined bring inner peace and love. These help to create the reality that you desire and keeping the balance of pure love here and now….

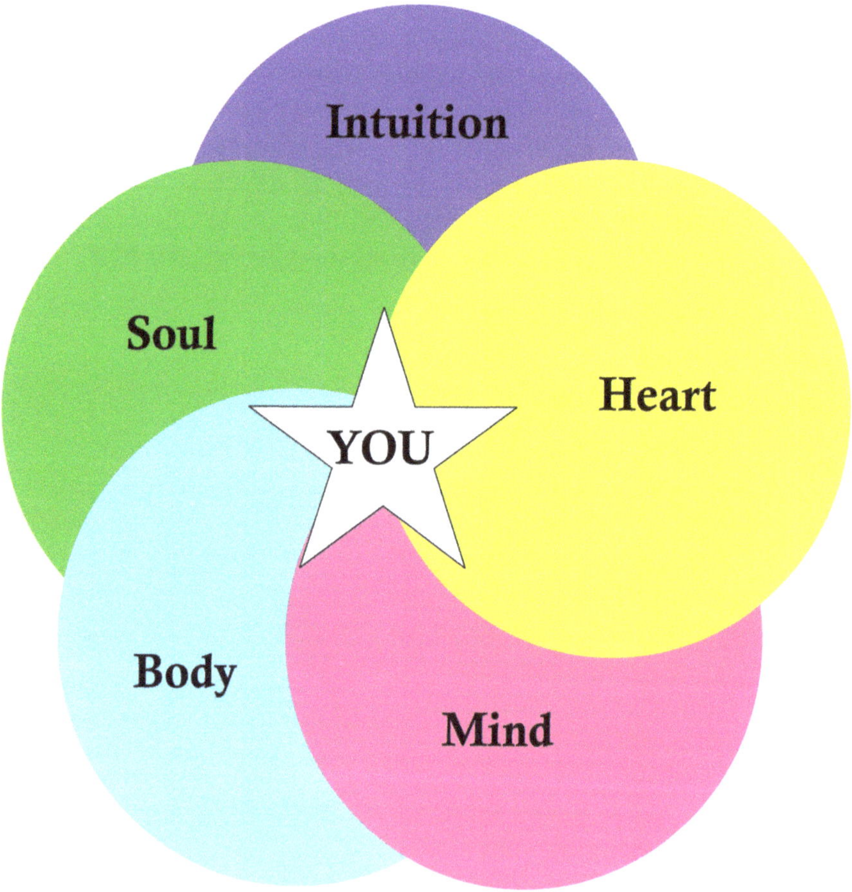

Intuition

Soul

Heart

YOU

Body

Mind

# Stage 3

## Working on self-love ingredients

Purpose of this stage is to focus on three points below through exploring and discussing ingredients of self-love.

1- Search for your true happiness …..within and reflected into your reality

2- Practice what we learned so far and get into more depth of the soul feeling, pure love you are created and the energy link to our creator in order to manifest it in outside world and create the reality we desire.

3- Start the planning of your future vision (family, money, health, life purpose, passion, carrier, friends, passionate love and anything that you desire to achieve in this life).

**Notes**

# Working on self-love ingredients

## To achieve self-love you have to have those ingredients:

| | Give one example for each ingredients how do you implement in daily? — Notes |
|---|---|
| **1** Have a vision of how you want to be and how your life want to be. | |
| **2** Be curious. | |
| **3** Be determent to be committed to what you agree with yourself. | |
| **4** Believe in yourself. | |
| **5** Love through desire your goals and purpose. | |
| **6** Be creative. | |
| **7** Be flexible. | |
| **8** Alloy yourself to be who you want to be. | |
| **9** Don't judge yourself, but be understanding towards yourself. | |
| **10** Show compassion to yourself. | |

# Working on self-love ingredients

## To achieve self-love you have to have those ingredients:

| | Give one example for each ingredients how do you implement in daily? Notes |
|---|---|
| **11** Experiment new things and unknown ways if it resonates with you. | |
| **12** Have discipline how to stick to your plans. | |
| **13** Be genuine. | |
| **14** Look for justice towards yourself and your actions towards others. | |
| **15** Stop being the victim but find ways how to notice the good things you have … focus on good things and be aware of things you don't like. | |
| **16** Be prepared to keep daily diary. | |
| **17** Willing to put yourself first. | |
| **18** Willing never to do to others what you don't like others to do to you. | |

# Working on self-love ingredients

## To achieve self-love you have to have those ingredients:

| | Give one example for each ingredients how do you implement in daily? | Notes |
|---|---|---|
| **19** Take responsibility for your actions and your happiness. | | |
| **20** Willing to learn to be master of observing what is happening around you daily. | | |
| **21** Create affirmations based on facts that you believe within. | | |
| **22** Willing to listen to yourself and only you to be in charge of your decisions and actions. | | |
| **23** Make notes daily what you learn from others and your daily experience. | | |
| **24** Willing to have daily conversations with yourself using techniques that you and only you create them and feel comfortable. | | |
| **25** Daily give love to yourself and make note of what you did. | | |

# Working on self-love ingredients

## To achieve self-love you have to have those ingredients:

| | Give one example for each ingredients how do you implement in daily? | Notes |
|---|---|---|
| **26** Your worries, fears, anxiety, insecurities, or any other emotions that you are experiencing have to be having daily conversation with your inner love in order slowly to turn into love and preparation for resilience on what to get more from this journey of life. | | |
| **27** Make time for you ….. alone time. | | |
| **28** Keep distance from people who don't make you happy or distract you from your goal and your purpose. | | |
| **29** Ask for help if you need it. | | |

# Working on self-love ingredients

## To achieve self-love you have to have those ingredients:

Whatever you do daily pay attention ….to learn, to enjoy it, to understand it, to appreciated, to accepted, to make changes if need it, to be grateful for you are and what you do, be your own critic, be open to listen to yourself if guidance are need it to change what you did not like, find out what inspired you, to be pure love and just notice anything thing that you notice.

**30**

| Give one example for each ingredients how do you implement in daily? | Notes |
|---|---|
|  |  |
|  |  |
|  |  |
|  |  |
|  |  |
|  |  |

*"Remember the reason you are in this life is to enjoy life and the only way to enjoy life is to connect to your pure love that you are born with and shine through the journey of life"*

*"No one is responsible for your inner peace and inner joy except for you." Debasish Mridha*

*"If you truly loved yourself, you could never hurt another".*
*BUDDHA*

*Remember:*
*A degree that distinguishes people in two categories is:*

*Diploma of happiness and harmony. ... who has this diploma is in the category of smart people and who have the ability to guide others to achieve happiness. .... this category has already tapped into their higher intelligence.*
*Those who have achieved this diploma are all of pure love and even in dark they will see and feel love..... ...*

So ask yourself questions blow:

Do you feel fulfilled and satisfied within all the times?

Do you have a clear plan on how you want to achieve what you want from life?

Do your goals bring justice and goodness to yourself and others in every action you make?

| Notes |
| --- |
| |
| |
| |
| |
| |

If you have these signs below it means that you have not reached the diploma of harmonization:

 Feel lonely when you are alone

 Don't have money and complain that don't have money. ..

 You are in relationship but not in love or single and satisfied, excite in true love

 Dream one day to get your dreams but do not have a detailed plan and starting point to start working on that plan

 Have sex without even when you are not in love

 Keep company only to push time and then get more unsatisfied that you spend time with out purpose or any satisfaction and you feel more bored by spending time with that company

 Talk about others with your friends but rarely for your real problems. ... or think about solving your problems but simply keep complaining

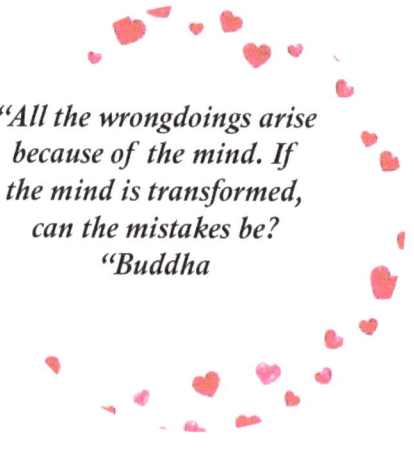

*"All the wrongdoings arise because of the mind. If the mind is transformed, can the mistakes be?*
*"Buddha*

**Exercise on self-love ingredients:** During the reading in silence your self-love ingredients practice the points below and make notes of your outcome for each ingredients.

## RDCHACVDPSEL

R..........Reflection
D..........Discussion with yourself and intuition
C..........Challenge the discussion
H..........Honest with yourself ...in order to know where you
         need improvements and what are your strength
A..........Analysis
C..........Conclusion
V..........Vision...visualise what you deciding
D..........Decide
P..........Plan in details
S..........Start
E..........Enjoy
L..........Love what you do with full passion

If things feel wrong then start the process from beginning...

| Notes |
|---|
|  |
|  |
|  |

*Time scale of learning up to here is three months.*

# Stage 4

to notice if they are ready to continue or do more work on previews stages.

1. The entry assessment

Test

of three previous stages.....

Recap......
a test

3. On their wishes and desires to achieve from working on MM

2. My observations during the first three stages

# Stage 5

## Momentum: first stage of MM in deeper level.

This stage is about connecting with your inner power, loving yourself, and writing your own life and making it happen. This is the chapter where all our bad or good experiences will happen; and if you are able to connect with your soul, inner self, and our creator, you will experience the magic of the moment, your blessings and you'll learn how to use your magic to create more magic around you. But if you cannot connect, then ask for help as you will be stuck in a continuous circle, unable to move onto the next chapter in your life. Open your heart and mind to the universe and try to recognise your true self (your soul), so you can get unlimited information back to you and become the master of your own life.

All the stages are linked and interconnected which means each client went through an individual and flexible journey, based on my skills and what the client offered at the moment. For details of each clients journey and on the work which has been done, refer to chapter seven of the book "Life is Magical... You are Magical". The methodology which I will explain below is fairly general and provides self-guidance for the reader, in order to help them achieve self-love. The guidance offered here is similar to that used on my clients during the research done on my second book, however the order varies depending on which stag the individual is and what is most useful at the moment.

"Success is to finding a way to be content in the present and having a clear vision of your desired future journey. Flexibility is a factor which contributes to success ... it is a part of growing and becoming wiser and wiser everyday, as a product of pure love"

# My skills are as follows (I gained these skills after becoming a product of love and finding the urge to see others around me happy, as it did not make sense that I was a product of love alone while others suffering around me. I asked the creator to give me the skills to help others and I had to be creative to know exactly what I required):

1. I connect with your soul (to know who you really are and what your purpose in life is) (This can be achieved through conversations with you), and feeling the energy of your soul.

2- I Understand who you are ... who you have become because of your life experiences...what has made you like that ... (through sessions we can discuss all that and understand it together ... to see if you like who you are or need to change in order to get what you want)

3. I have a deep understanding of your actions.... Are they created to survive? Are all actions based on your survival mechanism? I can help you to let go of your survivor mechanism so you can be able to enjoy life and not feel the need to survive. We are not here to survive but to enjoy life, this is the main purpose of the creator and you can prove it after you achieve your self-love. It is only when you have achieved self-love that you'll be able to see things clearly.

## Self-love in my theory is:

Someone who values themselves (it means accepting who you are and allowing yourself to think and plan, in order to be the best you can be), respects themselves (it means in any situation you should respect the idea of acknowledging your feelings, listening to yourself, and liking your qualities, actions, and achievements. Even if you think you don't like your qualities, you must still respect yourself and allow yourself to change those particular qualities), listen to yourself (make time to sit down alone and have a conversation, this could be; an evaluation of the day, reflection on certain situations or caring for your emotions, changing your thoughts/actions, or just saying nice things to yourself and praising yourself for any achievements), caring (caring is a very important word, as you need to care for yourself as you are looking after a baby or a child), allow yourself to dream and be the best you can be (it means setting yourself high standards so you can fulfill your goal and dreams, then making plans on how you're going to make it happen. Don't give up on your dream just because it needs time or hard work. If you truly believe in your dream and want to make it a reality, it is worth the time and effort on order to make it happen).

Time is the key to making those things happen, so think about where you have been spending your time until now, and what changes you can make in order to find time for yourself and the earlier points I mentioned.
Holiday alone can be a healing experience, as you have time dedicated to yourself, which you could use to complete the earlier points and subsequently organise how to continue them in everyday life.
There is so much more you can do to show love for yourself, but those are the main points I believe will help you discover what else you need during the process.
(Remember it took me more then one year to discover how to do it for myself ... in my first book I explain exactly how to do it and how did I personally did it ... everyone is different and require unique ways to discover it for themselves in order to make it work.)

# Stages to go through are:

1- To understand it ...and know exactly why it is important and how it works

2- Identify how to discover yourself, which techniques or methods work for you, as we are all different and required individual, tailored methods.

3- How to keep practicing self love (I do it daily, weekly, monthly and yearly .... a holiday alone)

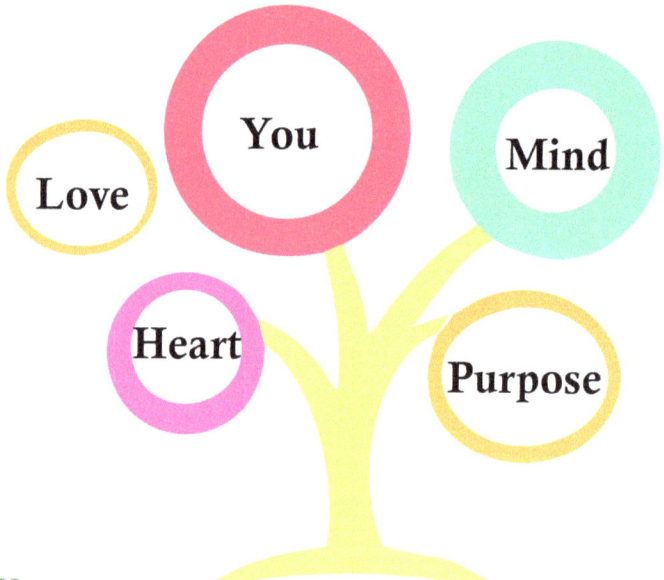

## YOU

In this session it is important to be in the moment in order to raise awareness of all the feelings you are unloading. My main focus is establishing a connection to the soul and creator, so that the client experiences energy within their soul. This in turn brings the focus to that feeling for few seconds, as the feelings are mixed with thoughts from the mind and feelings from the heart.

During this session it is important to tailor the exercises around the questions below and to the clients individual situation. The importance of these exercises it that they help the individual search for answers, as they are under the influence of their soul. These answers and discoveries can then be reflected upon at a later time. For example, client one had noted that her wish was to write a book as well as helping people in war torn countries who were suffering. However, the client had forgotten about that wish and could not recall writing those answers on the form, during the first session.

Who is who. ..
What is what...
Where is where ...
All what matters is knowing:
Who you are
Where you are now
Where you want to be and how you will get there
What you're going to do about being where you are and going where you want to be...
How you can be happy exactly where you are and appreciate what you already have ...
What you need to change in order to notice the good things that surround you at that moment ...

"Live like it is your last day,
Like it is the best day to create your future ...
Like it is the last day to be the best you can be and breath, feel, love , live "

## Mind :

At this stage we have to be aware of our thoughts, observe, reflect and show compassion and understanding. Because they are your thoughts at this stage.

| Notes |
|---|
|  |
|  |
|  |

## Purpose:

This is about you; what you want, where you are at the moment and what actions you have taken so far to accomplish your goals and move closer towards what you want. What can be done? Where should you start? So the work is centred around those questions.

| Notes |
|---|
|  |
|  |
|  |

## Heart:

We have to be aware of our feelings, observe, reflect and show compassion and understanding. These are your feelings which are truly sensitive. We have to show love, care, be active listeners. We also need to be reflective and analyse our feelings and the emotions we experience.

| Notes |
| --- |
|  |
|  |

## Love:

We have to work with our understanding of the individual link to love. We then subsequently bring these ideas into the bigger picture regarding how we want to be loved, from who we desire love and finally how we can make that happen. At this stage all of the participant who took part in the research were quite oblivious to the term 'self-love' however, the participants were surrounded by or experienced universal and passionate love. Consequently, all the individuals were facing the problems discussed in chapter seven.

| Notes |
| --- |
|  |
|  |
|  |

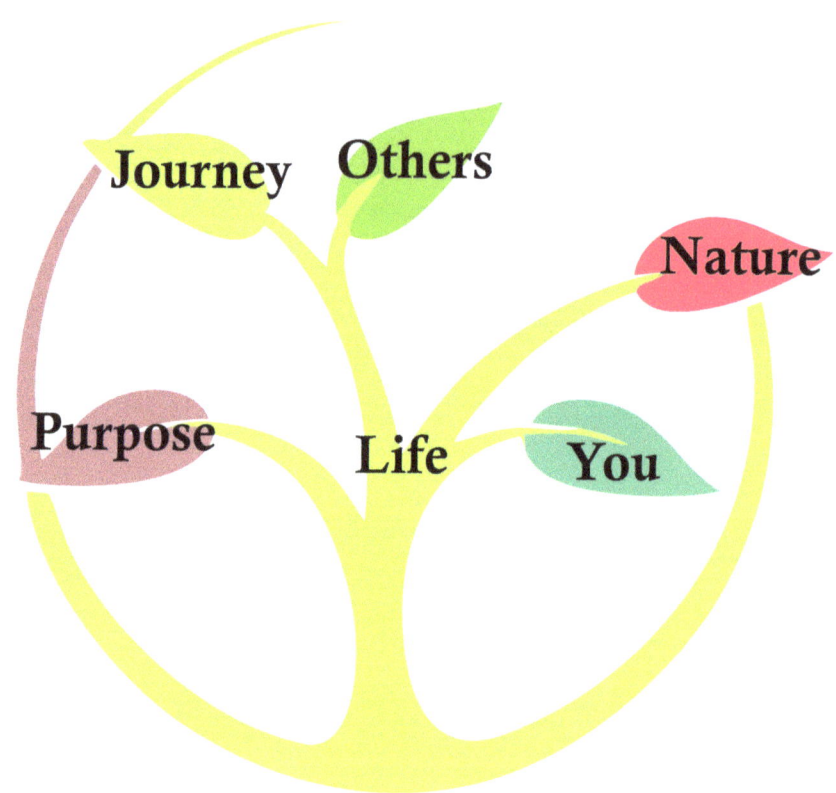

## LIFE

How do you perceive life? What is the meaning of life? How do you want your life to be? How has it been so far? I would suggest making notes and working with a diary because everything is a new journey which can easily be forgotten. The other benefit of a diary is that you become creative through your resilience of discovering and understanding yourself on a deeper level.

## YOU

The focus will be on the client at that particular moment, they must seek answers about what they are doing to satisfy themselves. This act of satisfying and making yourself happy must be explored.

# NATURE

At this point, we go back to childhood and incorporate the nature debate. We look back and explore your childhood and your connection to nature because is an important part of discovering your true self and gaining self-love, as nature has the power of producing love and guiding you to become product of love.

## OTHERS

We explore the role of others in your life and allow ourselves to be observers of our thoughts and feelings towards the role of others in your life.

## JOURNEY

It is important to stop time and reflect back on your journey until now, reflecting on the here and now as we'll as your entire childhood; a vision of your journey.

## PURPOSE

Once again Purpose is crucial, this time it is linked to the focus on others, on nature, on your journey and finally on yourself. These factors are all intertwined and provide a different angle from which you can analyse and reflect on your purpose. The key point is that you must ensure that you keep digging at a deeper level and continue practising being observer of your thoughts and feelings.

# LIFE

These questions all allude to a purpose which is centre around you. This helps you to connect more and more with your true self and discover how you can be you without it conflicting with your thoughts and your feelings. This, it is primarily about figuring out who you are and who you want to be.

| Exercise | Answers |
|---|---|
| How are you going to blend with life? | |
| How are you going to manage it or achieve it? | |
| How do you affect your situation? | |
| How do others affect your situation? | |
| How does the length of the journey affect your fulfilment of the purpose? | |

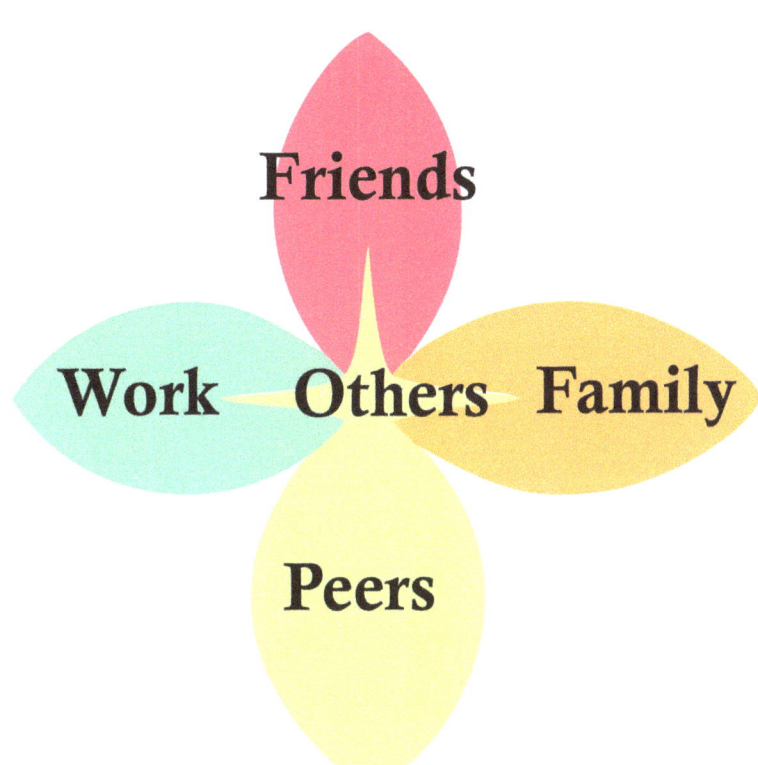

The role of others in your life is important, particularly when you don't have self-love and rely heavily on being loved by others (universal love or passionate love). That survival mechanism is costing you your happiness and keeping you away from your true self. Therefore, by exploring the role of others and raising awareness of the link between self-love, universal love and passionate love, you finally become familiar with your true self and understand the importance of knowing yourself.

"By accepting yourself and being fully what you are, your presence can make others happy."

(Jane Roberts)

# Mind

How we process information?

How we store information?

How we collect information?

| Notes |
| --- |
| |
| |
| |

The process of reprogramming your mind takes a minimum of six months after you have connected to your true self (the soul) and you are practicing self-love. When you work with your mind you have to raise the awareness of all your thoughts including those which you have repressed. This can be achieved through various techniques, which are tailored to meet the individual's needs. The steps are simple and the techniques include; spending time alone, making notes, having deep conversations with yourself that lead to a decision and attending coaching sessions at least once a month in order to reflect on your techniques and the methods that you are using. You become a master of your mind while caring for your thoughts through the process of reprogramming them. Thoughts have incredibly great power if we are not connected to our true self and if we create our reality based on our thoughts. On the other hand, if we are connected with our true self and still allow our thoughts to interfere in our life, it will create conflict which results in confusion and leads to various emotions. If these emotions are not a product of love then they could result in physical illness.

"Self-love requires you to be honest about your current choices and thought patterns and undertake new practices that reflect self-worth."
(Caroline Kirk)

"First of all, a soul is not something that you have. It is what you are."
(Jane Roberts, Seth Speaks: The Eternal Validity of the Soul)

# Body

Looking after the body is crucial and a way of respecting ourselves. This means that food, drink, exercise, sleep, inner balance and anything we put into our mouth and bodies must be considered carefully. This helps you serve the purpose of your soul. If you aren't satisfied with your body, are unhealthy, or if you damage your body, all other parts are affected. This in turn leads to unhappiness. As I explained previously, the body is also affected by the energy you feed it, based on the emotions from the heart. You can maintain a healthy body by producing love from the soul, eating healthily and doing regular physical activity. The soul is who we are ... it is the pure love. The mind on the other hand is who we have become based on the information we have acquired throughout our life. The heart is the organ which produces emotions from our thoughts and our soul, which in turn will spread the energy of those emotions throughout our body.

Raising the awareness of this whole process enables you and the client to recognise the importance of self-love and consequently fuels their desire to create ways of achieving it.
"Suffering is not good for the soul, unless it teaches you how to stop suffering. That is its purpose." (Jane Roberts, Seth Speaks)

## Heart

**Feelings (Exercise):**

**What are you feeling right now?**

Notes

It is important to take time to explore and understand your feelings. The process of healing your heart takes a minimum of one year. It involves learning how to do therapy sessions with your heart at least once a day, during the time you spend alone.

The heart is a very special organ and requires more attention than any other part of us, as it is very sensitive. It is also demanding on what it feels and takes time to accept and process new feelings. This can cause a bit of a mess if you are not organised, disciplined, and not guided by your true self (the soul, the pure love). For further details and insight refer to chapter seven of the book "Life is Magical ...You are Magical", which focuses on client one and explored how the process has worked.

"Falling in love you remain a child; rising in love you mature. By and by love becomes not a relationship, it becomes a state of your being. Not that you are in love - now you are love."
(Osho)

## Thoughts

Do we choose our thoughts?

How can we choose our thoughts?

Do we organise our thoughts?

How can we manage our thoughts?

Exercise, at this time of your life, which thoughts are you swimming in?

**Notes**

By exploring these questions, we gain insight into the ways in which we can master our thoughts and the ways we can care for them. We discover how to be our own therapist, our own spiritual guidance and how to prepare ourselves for new thoughts.

**Experience/event/present**

What is really happening in your life? Describe. The ultimate goal is to help people describe their life right now.

How is it affecting them?

Notes

Usually I do this in a very natural way, whether it be while walking, in a relaxed area, during the lunch, the whole point is ensuring that the client feels free and connected to their true self. This enables the client to reflect on what they are saying and come up with their own analysis, options, desires, solutions, strengths. This process will ultimately strengthen their self-love; their inner power.

Nature time allows you to be in a place of tranquillity and peace, which permits a person to reflect upon their recent actions and evaluate how life is going for them. This time is necessary in planning how to live your life.

Poets such as William Blake believed that humans are meant to live in nature and only then can their inner child be released. In nature we are able to have visions about how our lives will pan out, which gives us guidance.

Most of my clients were emigrants who were overwhelmed by various issues and problems. These individuals somehow found and gravitated towards me. At the time, I was simply going with the flow, and was not sure whether these individuals would be a part of. Although I did ask for permission to use their cases as part of the research, I was not clear about what kind of research and how I would go about it. For that reason, I was simply exploring anything that I found interesting and that I believed would bring peace and love to the world. I truly believe that it was meant to be as the clients had found me and were very open and honest from the start. They trusted me immediately, which is why I was able to offer help to my clients, even more than what they initially expected. This is evident in their feedback in chapter seven.

If the client is not honest, I cannot give them the help they require. This is because it is always their choice, which means that if they chose not to be honest, they are not ready to ask for help. Consequently, I am unable to help them. The law of the universe means that even if I attempt to help those who are not honest, it will not benefit them in any way.

At the time, I decided that I wanted my research to be based on the circle shown below. I found that the way the circle operates, was a root of unhappiness. However, as I progressed in the research journey, I discovered that self-love was the key to everything and the solution, which could lead to a world of peace and love.

My reflection of this circle is noted below. I found that a number of the participants were a part of the circle. I have analysed the circle on a deeper deep level in order to understand it personally.

**This circle below demonstrates an immigrant's journey:**

Client -emigrant-uk law-people-politics-action towards law- people - homeoffice -organisations (charity organisations)-other departments -solicitors- client- homeoffice -case worker- solicitor-interviews-refusal- solicitor- client alone… possibly challenge the decision -court- lose- turn back after all that painful journey and the hope gone down the drain.

I would like to have a deeper understanding of the whole circle and the questions below...at a later time:

How much money goes into this circle?
Who is benefiting?
Who is the main target?
What is the client benefiting from it?

The clients who were a part of that circle were experiencing severe depression, and suicidal thoughts (some even attempted suicide). Some were victims or perpetrators of domestic violence and others were involved in arranged marriages etc. Thus, the clients all had bleak pasts, characterised by pain and suffering. Not much had changed throughout their lives, they were still experiencing similar pain and suffering as a result of their emigration status. They do not feel stable or secure enough to start working towards their dreams or to look forward to good things. The future did not matter to them because they struggled to find the strength to think in a realistic way. There were only two ways in which they could think about their future, one was to create the ideal future in their head or alternatively they could remain in a cycle of depression, failing to see the link between their ideal future and their reality.
It is so easy to want your dreams but far more difficult to start moving towards them. You'll find any excuses not to do it. The word "want" and "can't because" are in constant conflict, which results in present disputes. The feeling of knowing that you want something, but convincing yourself that you can't have it and you start moaning about it, blaming others, thinking some people are lucky whereas you are not lucky, etc...

The more I worked with the clients, the more convinced I became that my theory was working. I saw great potential within each client, and they knew deep down inside them that they had the potential to live their ideal life. However, some of the clients did not follow up through the process below for a number of different reasons (refer to chapter four and seven for more details).

It is vital for them to understand who they are deep down, the real them. This means getting some spiritual help to them connect with their soul, such as the program I offered called "Heal yourself while you write your book". This helped individuals heal from the past, live in the present and plan for their dream future. This is achieved by acknowledging the souls voice and the language of pure love, so that next time you hear it, you can distinguish it from the voice of your mind (it's your head, logic, and others perspectives of who they think they are), heart (the emotions created based on thoughts, sensitivity, craving love and other emotional needs) and body (it is the gut feeling, as the soul tries to talk to you through your heart, your body, and intuition).

It starts with therapy (They have to do at least 80% of the work), then coaching (digging deeper into their soul...helping them listen to themselves and discover their potential, and then mentoring them through a form of spiritual guidance that resonates with them...flexible holistic guidance with a clear plan.

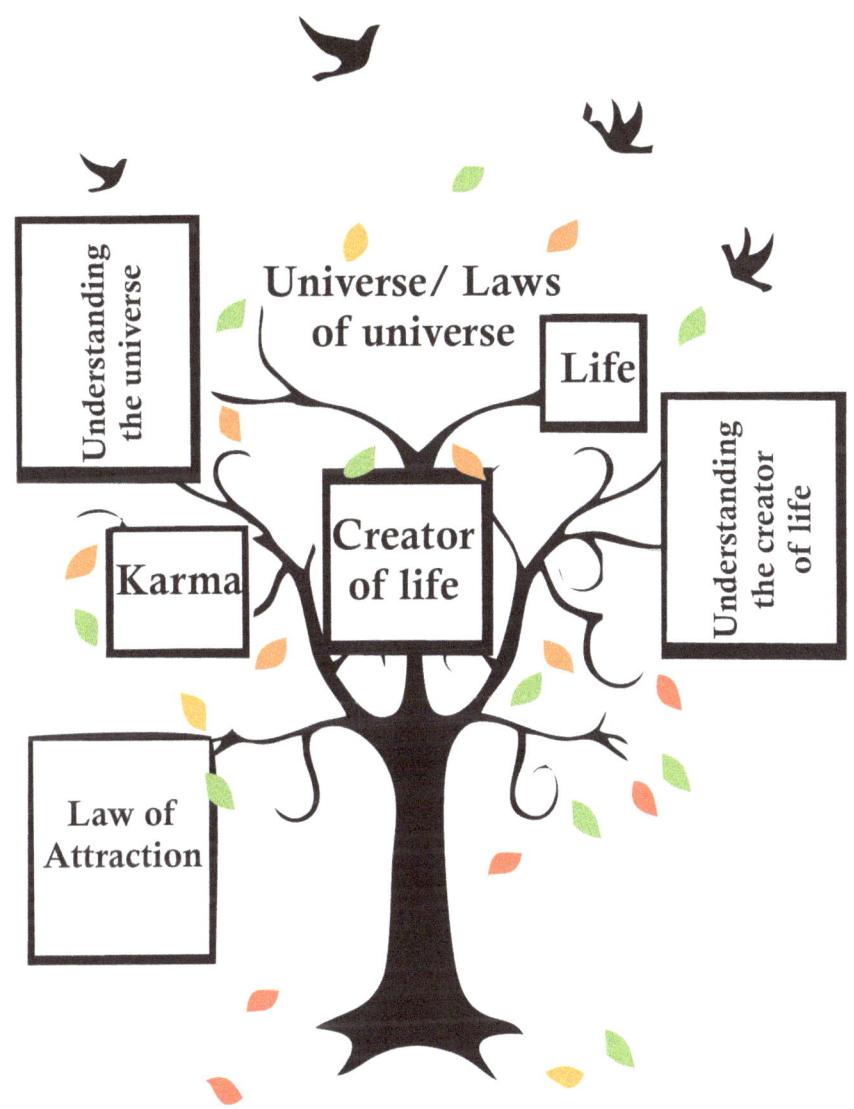

Three main rules that help you understand points below are:

1-Love your self how your inner child wants to be loved
2-Treat others the way your inner child likes to be treated
3-Do your best on everything you chose to do

It is crucial that you understand the above points, as everything is connected and links back to them including; our reality, who we are and who we became. All these points can be explained through a one day workshop or a one to one session in the language of the individual referring to their life experiences, actions, beliefs and their childhood life.

You must first begin by bettering yourself as a person, as you are aiming to be a role model to those around you. This means that you should treat the people around you in a respectful manner, so that your positivity can spread from them to others. This can be done through various techniques including taking a moment to breathe and thinking about how you want to be treated at that moment then acting accordingly.

In order to truly embrace self-love, you first must accept who you really are. You must not allow others to dictate your life for you, and the only decisions that you should make are the ones that you believe are right for you.

This process will allow you to understand who you are and you will get to know the real you far better. This will allow your self loving to come to fruition.

### Self-Love Break Down

- How to achieve 80% self love

- How to achieve 20% self love

- How to combine the 20 and 80 percent in order to achieve 100%

It is very important that you listen to your inner child when trying to get the other 20%. Your inner child reminds you to have fun and to stay in touch with the imagination you once had that lead you to be here. This imagination is the epitome of the 20% as it's all about being creative and unique.

This is all about self-love. Therefore we need to love ourselves how we deserve to be treated. We are all kings and queens and we must treat our sacred selves as well as you treat any human on this planet. We must not out everyone's needs ahead of our own as that could causes complications in the future, because we fail to meet our needs as human and we won't function at our best.

### Nature/Nurture

Understanding nature helps you understand yourself.
Understanding nurture you are able to connect to your soul and feed it.
Also make sure you begin to love yourself through alone time. Get to know what makes you happy and treat yourself
We can give ourselves that much needed day off or say no to the person asking you to do something you don't want to do. Think about you sometimes in order to feel at your best
"Nature helps us to understand that we have everything we need just were we are and have ability to create the reality we want.......just need to have deep and long conversations with nature around what I said"
This has helped the client to be more aware of their intuition, their inner voice and to take time to breath-reflect-analyze-and come to decision based on pure love for themselves and others- take action towards the goal created by the soul. Moreover it helps them to be their own healer through conversations they have with their human parts, such as heart, mind and body but mostly is heart that need more healing then anything. (for more information refer to client one how she has managed to achieve the transformation through magical module).

### Survival exercise

Stranded on a tropical island, alone with nothing but nature to help you survive. 95% of the population are not fulfilled. And just survive in terms of love, by giving them this exercise it may stimulate their inner power and take their attention away from surviving, to bring it to the moment. Right here right now to love.

# Stage 6:
# Acceptance

Learn to accept where you are in order to allow yourself to find positives on your situation, and raise your awareness on negatives in order to have clear vision of how you want to spend each moment and how you want your future to be.

On this stage I worked with clients to accept what was done on momentum stage and more as we go through the acceptance. Acceptance is a very important stage as you need to have lots of conversation with yourself through the love you have within that we have explained and gone through on momentum stage. Through the conversations you will learn a lot about the power of pure love, the power of the moment, the power of the time and how to share love and care with others.

"The real success is about being content exactly where you are and having clear vision of how you want your journey to be .....this will lead to enjoying each moment and working towards your vision but the most fascinating thing is that your vision will get bigger and bigger as you grow being fulfilled exactly where you are and with what you have ... this can happen only by having ingredients of pure love ... Moreover, you will never be afraid of death because you lived fully in moment,  you did your best, you achieved to make yourself happy and have courage to go for your vision and you will know that next journey in the future life will be much easier as you have overcome all you challenges and got in touch with pure love that will follow you whatever you go ... even after you die ... even in another life journey that you will be ... life is magical ... we are magical " "Your purpose is actually quite simple, it's to look deep into yourself, into your soul, and your childhood memories can help you to do that.

To discover and nurture, who you truly are, to know and love yourself at the deepest level and to guide yourself back home when you lose your way. The more you do this, the more aware and present you become, which creates more harmony in your life… Your self-worth has nothing to do with your craft or your calling and everything to do with how you treat yourself. Loving and accepting ourselves even when we fail miserably because love is what can heal anything and guide you to feel fulfilled and loved"

## Self-love guidance :

1-justice towards yourself and others

- So do things that you like others to do for you ….do it for yourself and do the same to others if you can if you can't at least don't do anything else …just walk away

2- Is accepting that you are protected. … just take time to be silent and sink in that you are alone in this life; that is for a reason. No one is to be blamed for your unhappiness, because you are your own boss; you are the creator of your own reality. You have free will and choice to make decisions, and, because you are alone that tells you that you are number one in this life. Your job is to satisfy yourself. Every decisions made should be for your own good.

Once you do that you can make happy people that you love also, so is important to make decisions that the purpose is to make yourself feel loved, fulfilled and satisfied with your decisions. Your purpose should be crystal clear that is all about you creating the reality you want through being fear, genuine, honest, straightforward, disciplined and product of love, of who you truly are.
No one can give you what you already have within and you cannot give to others love because of the free will and free choice everyone has to discover it for themselves and the they can share it with others or guide others how to discover it.

117

It is very important to understand that love cannot be given to others because it does no good to them apart from it makes them attached to you which is not right thing to do as you prevent them from discovering their own pure love but instead they become attached to your pure love.

Don't forget, life can be fulfilled without having nothing if you have self-love. Exactly at that point you start to see all the colours of life. Important is to notice and see all the colours of the life through pure love and that it does exist to each individual and the life around. It's those colours that brings joy, happens, true universal love , true passionate love, and help you to have the reality you desire, such as money, fame, etc. If you don't have self-love you cannot see and notice the colours it does not matter what you have in this life. Only self-love can bring the colours crystal clear to see, feel and dance with them. Don't mix colours with money, fame, sex, or other excitements you get form material things because those what you see from short pleasure are just shadow of the real colours and can cost you more as they make your life journey more difficult and complicated. Material life does not bring the colours to your life but it does help if you have your self-love as you can use what you have wisely and enjoy the colours of your life journey. Colours are product of pure love. Pure love is your soul. Your soul is who you are, that never dies and have all the answers you need to know.

**Staying still**

Importance of staying still everyday for few minutes at least,
How to use stillness,
How to discipline yourself to make it a routine,
The benefits. (Staying still helps you to notice things that usually don't notice, to hear yourself and universe and creator).

**Notes**

Staying still - important of staying still for few minutes every day helps you to connect with your true self beyond your human parts, such as mind, heart and body. Connecting to your soul and to see things through pure love which is you, is your soul and it gives you that fulfilment and reminder of who you are and how to see life. How to use stillness? Stillness can be used as a starter at least 30 minutes everyday and then through practice you can learn how to be in that mode automatically any time you choose whatever you are doing. Stillness can be pointed to your direction of your problems also with the practice in order to see the problems through your pure love and serve the purpose you are searching link to the problem you bringing to the stillness.

To hear yourself and creator for guidance

Feel loved

Produce love

The benefits are:

Staying still helps you to notice things that usually don't notice,

Becoming pure as whole you including everyday actions towards yourself and others through reflection – analysis- decisions-planning

## Hearing

In relaxation mode you start hearing different voices in your head and outside your head.

How to learn to recognise the voices where they are coming from and how to communicate with them,

Types of different conversations we can have in our hearing relaxation mode,

Hearing what you usually don't hear...hear the silence.

Hearing is a great skill and is in different levels, but the first level is to hear your soul, your true self, your pure love and slowly you take it from there going up to levels until you achieve fully yourself love. And then you learn how to listen to the creator in order to get guidance to get the reality life you desire. The purpose of the creator is for everyone to be in peace and love while they enjoy the magic of life that surrounds them. It is a theory and fact that we born and die, also is a fact that babies are full of pure love and children until age of 25 they still have some percentage of pure love. The difference between they have and they are pure love is that when children get influence by the information's they have been feed it through life experiences and people it moves them away from their pure love that they have been born. Creator has given free will and free choice which mean we can chose who to follow. To follow our mind, our heart or our soul, we have not been taught how to be us, how to connect with our soul because the soul has not been proven that it does exist. For that reason things get messy when it comes to understanding happens and what makes us feel fulfilled and loved. It is very simple ... just be who you are ... be product of pure love....and follow the structure of magical module to help you create your own techniques and methods how to be you ... how to be product of pure love....how to connect to your soul and how to be guided by your soul in order to feel loved and fulfilled exactly where you are and then you will be able through your soul guidance to give love to others who need.

To share your love with others and to achieve the material life you desire. This is simple, achievable and enjoyable. Only thing that will stop you to be guided by your soul is your mind and heart that has limitation to what they know and the don't have ability to know how to show pure love to yourself and others. The mind and heart are not able to be genuine with you and others because if they are it means you are fulfilled and loved exactly where you are and you never do any harm to anyone including yourself. Moreover you will be product of pure love and you will help others to become product of pure love. This was the reason why few of participants in this research where unhappy and did not follow the process until the end as you can see on chapter seven and four of the book "Life is Magical…You are Magical".

### Smelling

- Through the smell we can allow ourselves to understand our likes and dislikes.

- To choose what we want to like and how to make it happen …

Strengthen our skills through the smells that we don't like by improving our weakness and through the smells we like to strengthen our strength by reminding us of the nice smells,

- Notice the smells we never noticed before so it helps us to understand better the universe, people and ourselves through the world of smells.

**Notes**

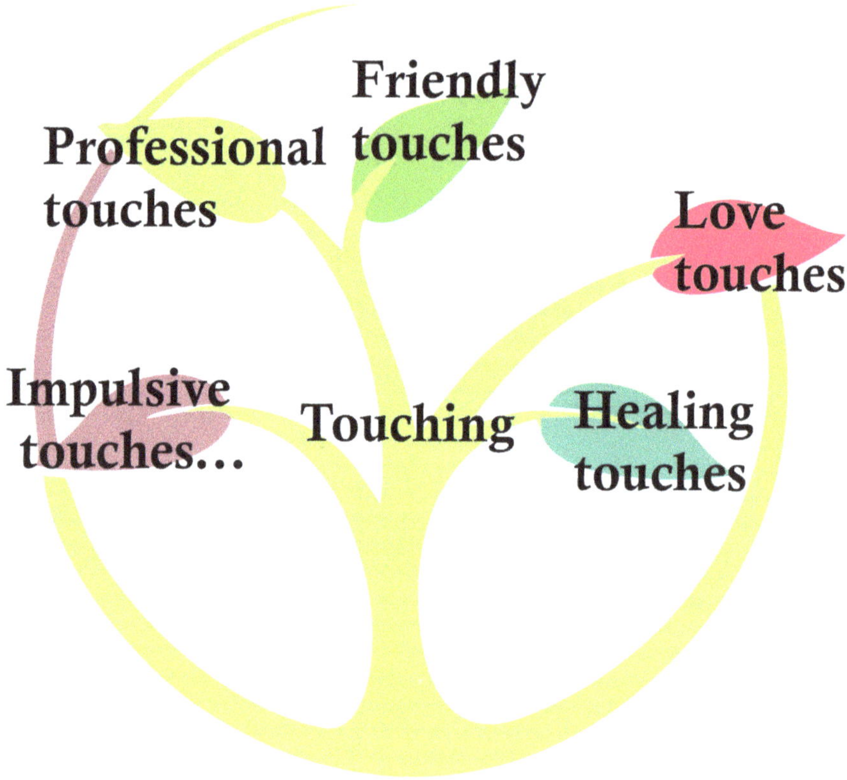

Friendly

Professional touches

touches

Love
touches

Impulsive

touches... Touching Healing
touches

How to apply to ourselves and others in order to serve us they way we want. (Touches are powerful tool that produce love ).

| Notes |
| --- |
|  |
|  |
|  |

**Observations**

Noticing
body
language

seeing

Seeing

Seeing
the nature
in relaxation
mode

The way
we see
different

Seeing

Seeing
through
eyes

"Every day if we sit and look at ourselves in the mirror, watching as a movie every day action that we make and understand what is the devil and what is goodness because eyesight is the look of our goodness ... sometimes we have power to we are lost in the sight of goodness ... but in these cases it is a little practical to look without silence in our own silence without paying attention to the minds but just looking at ourselves in the depth of our eyes a few second until we connect with the good ... you understand when you are tied because a smile may arise or a pity or a cry of ignorance you have lived without realizing the true value of yourself .... or a critical one ... such a love ... or many things can happen when you connect with your goodness " This exercise helps in your relationship with the soul ..... with your inner goodness. ... with what you are really. ... with your power to give kindness to yourself and others :) .

Because I think it's the soul ... your light that is immortal ... have you been immortal ... light, energy, kindness to accompany us in all the life we do and at that time we pass to the universe when a schematic has begun a life. ... It is love that cleanses the mind, heart, and body ... is the love of the soul to learn to speak the language of love even when others speak the language of love because with the language of love helps and heals everything that comes into contact .... It is exactly that language of love that guides you to accomplish the fulfilment where you are going to be missing nothing. ... to feel at ease and to enjoy everything that makes you feel comfortable and smile and to smile. ... to be in love with yourself and your life that you smile all around you and understand those who do not speak the language of love .

**Noticing unseen things (exercise)**

Noticing unseen things

Do exercise through mindfulness

Notice feelings-make note of them

Your thoughts -make note of them

**Notes**

**Hearing sessions:**

How do we view things?

Ask question and we get three different answer within or maybe four ....

1-answer from the soul

2- answer from the heart

3- answer from the mind

4- sometimes the body gives as the answer also depending on the health of our body. ... if the body is healthy will be silence and follow our decision.

What is the right answer? How would we know?

**Notes**

If you want to hear and feel your soul, stay away from people who have not achieved self-love, walk in nature, give lots of hugs to your self and nature, smile in mirror to yourself and nature, dance and have fun with nature, be grateful to the creator for what you have.

## Mindfulness exercise

Mindfulness exercise to do at home or create your one

How to create routine once a day to be mindfulness in the things we need to focus or just reflect.

Things we need to be happy and content / How can we manage to have them or get them.

Notice feelings ...make note of them

Your thoughts ..make note of them

Your communications

# Notes

Example mindfulness will help the clients that don't appreciate things that they have but their focus is more on how to get their illusion life or dream life quick and easy way through others and not through working for it one step at the time.

Few of the reasons people are not honest with themselves and others: (example migrants who migrate to other countries for better life and safety they experience some or all the points below)

They feel embarrassed to tell the truth about their life.

They don't want to feel weak.

They don't want others to know their pain and their suffering.

They are not aware that telling the truth is a start to get the purpose they are perusing.

They are terrified to expresses what they are going through as they are afraid they will not be strong enough to continue.

They are confused and they don't take time to stop and talk to what they are experiencing.

They live in shadow.

They live in illusion that does not exist and they walk away from the truth.

They talk about others so they don't have to confront their own problems.

All this individuals that are part of that list they are so lost and in deep depression, most of them are young parents and so on life goes on..... when very simple can be turned into joyful and happy life by being product of pure love towards yourself and others which starts with being true to yourself and confronting everything guided by the soul.

Sometimes there are people who want help but are not ready to be pure person because they don't believe that being pure is the first step to build the journey they want. So I teach all those techniques and methods but they still try their old habits and make things worse for themselves. I know that I have to give them a chance to show the options as it is the reason they entered my life but still they need more work on understanding of the conflict between their thought, feelings and the importance of self-love. As easy can be confused self-love with narcissist and egoist for those who have not achieved the self love. The difference is that the person who have achieved self love can never be egoist, narcissistic or any negative words or things because is pure love. Self-love is showing yourself how to produce love and how to be the real you "the pure love".

"If you feel fulfilled where you are ....you will know how to help others automatically and you see the love in everything"

" The only knowledge you need to know on this life is how to make yourself fulfilled, be in peace and in love with yourself and life"

And, if you have not found happens within... then you cannot found it in long term nowhere......those happiness in short term (objects, money, sex, family, others, fame , excitements ) are short and will not be with you when you are alone in your quite time .... and... that's why you avoid the time alone because you don't want to confront it ... as it is deep level ... is beyond our livings. ... is what I experienced when I was 7 that through my pain I discovered this big power of love. ... and I reinforced when I was 18 and 36 ... now I just enjoy it ... now I sit on it as I do what I have to while I am here as human and enjoy all those things that human has opportunities to do and enjoy ...
So ... I started with momentum. ..pain , - Acceptance. ..that I am here I want to find way to understand it and enjoy it - goal. .....to be product of pure love, inspired through nature to keep enjoying the beauty of life, committed to be loved and share love and get my vision of the reality I want, affirmation of whole who I am and what I do, love ... be love.

" Someone who don't knowledge who they are for themselves they can never knowledge who others are because they become others ... others become perception of others .... perception of others are just thoughts created from someone who has not found themselves .... and that's why the world is based on ... and we die without noticing ourselves and the magic of life. "

"The soul does not know gender, does not know places, does not know colors, does not know objects or looks because is energy based on love "

Again time-to-time you have to keep asking yourself the questions below until the answers you got you have achieved it. So by asking those questions time to time you reinforce the answers, get closer to your true self and get in touch with the feeling of pure love and self-love.

**You need to ask your self :**

-Who you are?

-Who you want to be?

-How you want your life to be?

- What do you need to make it happen?

 The life you want

- What is the meaning of love for you?

- How would you like your partner to be? And are you like that? If yes you are ready to meet someone like that if you are not then you need to work with yourself.

- Can you live alone? Why not? But are you happy if you are with the wrong person? What do you need to do to find the right person for you?

Answers

129

My reply to one of the clients while he was living on his illusion vision and did not want to allow himself to be in present and make the link between present and his illusion vision.

"Me and you we have talked and now I think you are in stage to learn to trust your purpose and discover yourself "who you really are? , what is your life purpose ? How can you start fulfilling your purpose? Do you like your purpose or do you want to change it? Again, keep going back to the question who you really are? Who you want to be ? How can you be who you want to be? And where can you start? " I feel that's your work for now and that's what you need to focus all your positive energy and allow time to feel all the negative emotions you are feeling "

What all it matters is everyone should put their energy and work into understanding what really matters !!!! And get it ...

Which for me since age of 7 was all about focusing how to be content and in love with myself that I was in this life and the life with everything provides. ... also once we discover that what we want automatically you will release that is about love - purity ..in order to get that .....which after you get it you well feel fulfilled, loved and in peace. ....during the journey you still will feel that way but because you are working on to become pure and practice purity in everyday life you will go through adventures. ...which you still enjoy it and learn from it as you grow inside you  every day.

.... one step closer to be you. ...and feel fulfilled, in peace and love. ... and with the work with the clients I point out when they are not being genuine with themselves and others in order to keep practicing the pure love as they say they have it but they are not aware of full picture and practice of pure love. Because they don't have self-love. If you don't have self-love you will never be genuine with yourself and others, you never can treat yourself right and others they way you like to be treated.

I lost my self trying to please others said client number one on chapter seven of the book "Life is Magical...You are Magical".

1- " As long as you look for good on you .....your universe will be your teacher "

2- "When you try to follow the purity you will never feel alone or out of purpose. ..."

3- " The change comes through your reflection of the conversation you have as whole you by being still. ....by sitting on your energy humbled in universe"

4- " The universe is everything and can be used in bad way or good way ....only the difference is that negative energy can never give you peace and love but the good energy will give you peace, love and fulfilments. ......... (the God, the religion are just roots to lead you to one direction. ...to understand universe. ...to understand how to use the universe as we have free will and free choice. ....to choose the good energy or the negative energy and is up to us which one we feed on us .....based on what we feed the energy thee reality will be created and our feelings. .....the feelings have power for good or bad)".

I learned that universe is the creator then only explanation I can give is that everything we create .....such as ...seeing spirits or communicating with angels or getting messages from other world and lots other things mire are just what we have asked universe to give us and with our determination and hard work we get those gifts ....... is all about energy and is universe our everything. ...we just have to choose which path to follow ...the good or negative and we have the ability to know and recognize those two ...that's why is our choice to choose and then all it starts in slow process depending on your determination, resilience, hard work, wiliness and the passion to love the purity.

"Again the learning for each individual is unique and different because of our free will and choice which makes us unique even though we all are energy and the energy is the same .....but how we choice to use it makes us unique "

131

Understanding and being aware
of different individual journey:
We can never know for sure
exactly why the life journeys
are different from each individual
but I think it is based on few
factors below:

Previous life consequences. ........
contract with
creator before we come to this life
as we choose based on our previous
life achievements and experience.

Foundation of reality at the moment ...
as that changes based on humans progress
/actions /thoughts/purpose/
connection to their soul etc

People who are lost but somehow
they lost their really hearing and
they all what they do is to survive
or end it all ....

The influence of pure human beings that try to make sense why they are in this reality and how they can make it happen their inner calling....their true path that they choose before they decided to come to this life.
What happen !!!

Those who controlled others because they cannot control their inner conflict.

Those who have worked hard to discover their inner power but instead they use it for main purpose to make money which takes them back further back before they started to work in their inner power ...

Guilty parents who just dig themselves in deep guilt everything they try to come out of it ....

Also the creator strategy to make as work hard to remember the benefits of being good , the good things others do to us , the good being power to everything, .....we easy remember bad things and how to act like that , as it is easy , it is short road and smooth compare to the road of being good is claiming mountains and with fall time to time but is peaceful, joyful, lovable. Is with the purpose that will take you for sure in top of mountains....even if it did at least you know you are in zone of your really purpose of getting closer to that .... mostly remember is not about getting in top of mountains but cleaning your human being and putting in same level with your soul .... Your soul is the top of mountains because that's the whole purpose of being in this life ....that is the test we have to pass each time we live. ..until we get in same level with our soul .... I am not sure how that can happen as it is very difficult thing to do and I am not sure what will happen after that can be achieved by everyone in this life ..... what will happen then !!! Maybe will be a peaceful life with full of love and then will start from beginning where all this started .... which mean will be a test to see how long will be until someone can poison society again ...

Does it take only one to poison whole us ? How easy is that to be done?

Very easy, because people think happiness comes from not working (it's easy working when love is not present as the focus will be on material things and not in love. ... Which makes you think that that's what you will get ... sometimes you do get it but it's too late .. .your life has almost end it when you realize that love was missing and you feel dry).

The good person, the person who does everything from foundation of love doesn't focus on material things but they just come part of love - plan-action-satisfaction-fulfilment-self-realization ...

As love is the key who can help you to open all the other doors by using the right tools. For the good person to change the society is harder because the good things are unseen ... you only can feel it , visualize it, and live it ...
-Spending time alone ... which helps you to be quite and listen to your soul, creator, any other spirit or energy that is trying to guide you (which could be any one ... loved ones that are life or dead ), universe, the whole you (mind , heart and body ... the body is the gut feeling ... which you can help you to listen to other parts of your body and connect with your own body). While you are in this state you make notes of anything that comes to you.....as later you forget ... make notes of feelings, hearing , words, and of your own thoughts and feelings ... as you may feel feelings that are not yours, may hear thoughts that are not yours, my hear words , sentences that never come across before etc ....

One of exercises I created for the client:
Two things to work on it this month:

1- To heal your heart (have free time with yourself and be mindfulness about how your heart is feeling, listen, understand it, care for it and show compassion )

135

2- Create affirmation to grow your confidence and believe in yourself example "I love ... (the name of client), I am very confident that I can deal with any situation, no matter what it is , I believe in myself , I can achieve my dreams".

Example when the client were more connected to the universe and creator:

The client at age 6 was very creative and very wise on the things was saying but as she turned 8 years old she got influenced by reality and was drown into the things her reality was presented and less listening to her inner voice.

Client one and client two said:

Before age 6 were very pure, genuine and connected with intuition and to nature.

Client one said that after age 7 up to age 13 used to be very active, had lots of courage and wanted to copy adults. She was experiencing it through role play, by playing with the doll and she was pretending to be the adult looking after the sick doll trying to take it to hospital. She was looking after the doll and now when she was remembering, was feeling it ....and she said "I missed my mother" ... as her mother was not part of her life as her parent were separated when she was very young. After age 14 up to age 18 she said got closer to her soul, started to follow the religions, read books, spend time with the horse. She could see beyond what was presented.  Age 18 up to 25 she got lost as started to understand people's actions and let them control her life as she was hiding for comfort in her special corner every time she was upset. My hidden corner provided everything I need it, she said. Was providing safety, comfort, I felt small and I felt rebelling towards what people were doing to me to show them that I could do it.  The marriage was another big confusion that took me in another path with my head down and I felt I was getting smaller and smaller every day.

My analysis of our conversation is that I see a child thrown into life without love and guidance how to produce love, how to gain self-love which lead to rebelling as expression of anger why she is not been valued and why she has to be controlled.

Similar thing happen to the client 14 (8 years old girl) that she experienced same feelings but her parent dealt with compassion through love. In one of our sessions she said "I want my way that's why I misbehave". I replied saying "is very good you have your own way but also have to listen to adults instructions and find way how to communicate your feelings and thoughts so you both can value and understand each other and find middle way for you best interest". She smiled.

Most of the clients have shown the same rebellions and the reason is they get lost in their emotions. Furthermore they are confused of the reality being surrounded. They use their rebellion to do stuff that really doesn't like it but somehow it excites them and brings satisfaction. To try to be happy is the road that has not been proven and not seen … and that's why they don't even try.

The moment is important, and you need to use all the stages of magical module in an authentic way in order not to be just illusion and not complete with the influence of the fear … "Moment is reflection of the individual".

# Stage 7

# Goal

To understand who you are at the present and to be conscious of the choices you make, you must ensure that you have a goal. Dream your wishes, visualise your dreams, and break up them in small goals.

We all wants wealth, health, fame, success, love, peace, harmony, to be surrounded by people who love us, to have the job we love to do and be happy, however, we all have to start with a vision, a plan, decisions, time scales, an action and starting point. We discussed momentum and acceptance and now we have a clearer idea about how to make the right decisions for ourselves and how to enjoy the journey from the starting point up until we reach the goal. This stage is about helping the client reflect, analyse, create and strengthen their connection with their soul/mind/heart/body, in order to obtain the reality they desire.

Refer to chapter four and seven regarding how the participants had worked through this stage and most of the client could not go past the goal stage. What I mean is that their goal was the end of the line and they wanted to skip the whole journey and reach the end line. They failed to truly work through the momentum and acceptance stage, as they were merely focused on entering the fast lane.

The topics below have been applied to the clients in personalised and unique ways. Below you will see the main topics that need to be expanded, based of the client's uniqueness.

## Answers

 **Imagination**

Imagination of when you are dead

What will happen at your funeral?

In 10 years time or when you are old. What will happen and how do you see it?

Imagination of your death, or what will happen at your funeral, or in 10 years time when you are a pensioner .... Make notes .... Re-read notes and then take more notes.

#  No limitations

The soul knows no limitations, (describe what the soul is and why it does not know limitations and why we use the word "can't" when the soul doesn't understand can't.

The soul has both free will and free choice. Our choices, actions, decisions and influences the decisions of karma and law of attraction (this is a fairly complex and unique theory which can be explained in a one day workshop).

It is only the mind, which has limitations.

Do meditation relating to the language of the soul, either a general one or one to one.

| Notes |
| --- |
| |
| |
| |
| |
| |
| |
| |

# Believe in yourself

## Answers

You can believe in the creator, but how can you believe in life, the universe and the creator if you don't believe in yourself?

What does it mean to believe in yourself?

How can we discipline ourselves to take the journey to achieving self belief? (An exercise with small steps which leads from the place the individual is currently at to the place they want to be in self love...to be in a workbook as an exercise).

#  What is love

Self love>universal love>passionate love (intimate love).

Self love (is believing in yourself, accepting yourself and where you are, taking time to understand yourself.

Being a great holistic facilitator to yourself (to question, to criticise, to discipline, empathise, love, care, to be kind, be understanding, a shoulder to cry on, be encouraging, treat your self, respect, forgive, remind yourself to live in the moment, help to follow the plan 80% and 20%).

Allowing yourself to be a unique version of yourself, find yourself by spending time with the whole you (soul, mind, heart and body).

| Notes |
| --- |
|  |
|  |
|  |
|  |
|  |
|  |
|  |

Goal exercise on self love

On top of this exercise to be the reason what is the whole purpose of them loving themselves?

Where that will take them and how ? In detailed plan journey from where they are and where they want to go.

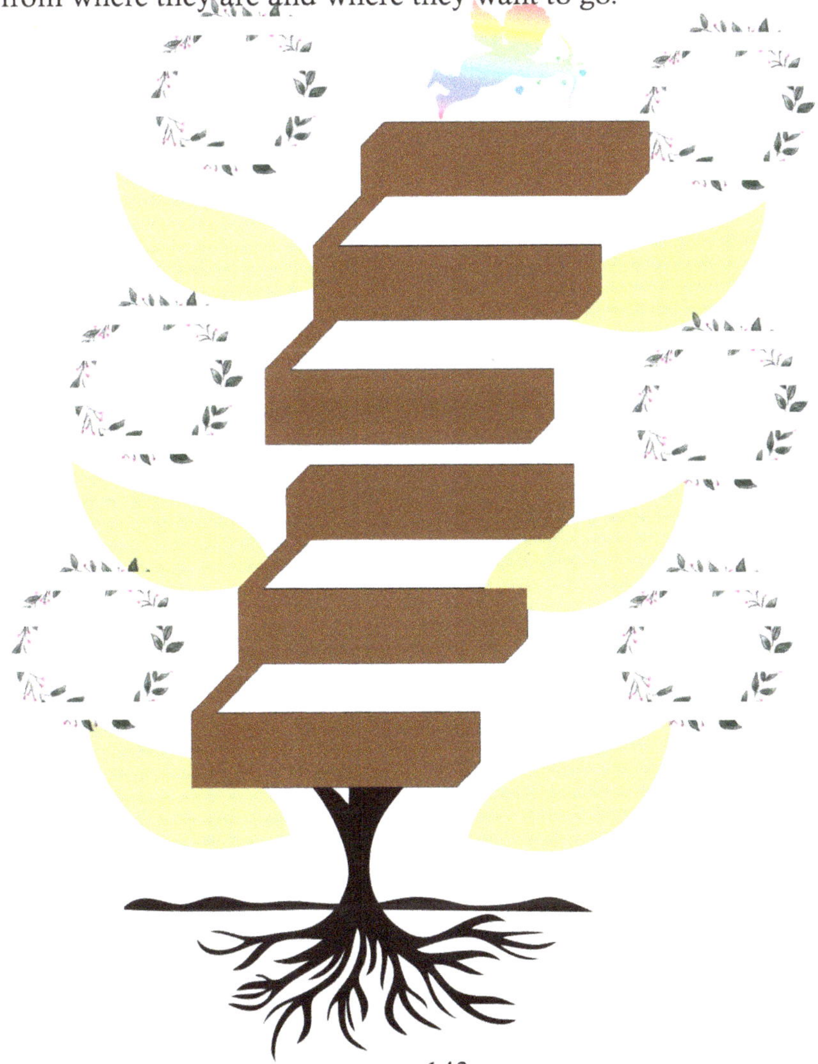

143

# Goal Steps

Example: My Goals ( individual creates their own goals which each goal have sub goals).

- I surround my self around people higher than me in the sense of self love achievement, self realization, fulfilment, criticism, speak up freely etc

- When I am around people that have to do with my work I make sure I have enough energy to be present and be there fully ...

- Family and friends that don't fit on the categories I mentioned then ...I will keep healthy balance where I benefit and they benefit. ...so we don't damage each other's. ...but we help each other to grow more ...

- I make sure use meditation, affirmation, magical module to keep me granted. In same time to feel light, so I am not independent from this life, but I can use this life to keep continuing being lighted. ...

Imagine this progression:

The individual (somewhere being alone without any help)-suffering-accepting-reason for purpose-goal-believe-inspire to feed the goal-determent-strength to fight-affirming-love.

"love yourself from the source of the soul and not from the ego of the overflowing cover of the diaphanous"

"Doing bad to others is enough even thinking about it, and it will come back to you what you do....even twice"

"Its not integrity others to save your life because you have to do it as it is your lessons and everything lies within you...be creative, curios and determent to create your own path"

Client one said: I never thought of You (myself) - Me (the ordinary one, the common one)-and space (vjollca).

| 1- For knowledge. . do you feel wiser and why? You are smart and why ? | 2- Trust ... how do you know how to believe? |
| --- | --- |
| | |

*As you are in that energy can you create 11 cards with the answers from each points below please, so you can have it and remind yourself anytime you feel the need too:*

| 3.Practicing self-confidence and self believe....how? | 4.Practicing God's Faith/will/guidance |
| --- | --- |
| | |

5. Daily plan, weekly and monthly plan...how can you?

6. How can you practice emptiness of Your Mind and letting go

*As you are in that energy can you create 11 cards with the answers from you of the points below please so you can have it and remind yourself anytime you feel the need too:*

7. How to reach the space, the universe?

8. The imagination of things that happen tomorrow ... how would you like to go tomorrow or the situation that will occur and how can you adjust it on your best interest? Based on pure love?

| 9. Weekly prayer. | 10. How could you learn from others? |
|---|---|
|  |  |

*As you are in that energy can you create 11 cards with the answers from you of the points below please so you can have it and remind yourself anytime you feel the need too:*

| 11. How to protect myself and enjoy the moment |
|---|
|  |

2. Apply the rules of the universe to be pure in heart and mind as you are in the spirit

3. Wish the best for others and do not let others hurt you.

1. Understand yourself

Walking on straight line towards purity, only the one who is determined to walk straight and is enthralled with the real listening can do.

4. Let go of those that don't fit on your energy.

5. Meditate regularly. .. at least once a day to continue to understand yourself .

6. Every day look at your day as in the movie to reflect and correct it.

7. I constantly recall that you are only important person in this life and this life is for you ... only you decides how to live and be responsible, don't blame others.

149

**If you do follow the steps mentioned in the right way, your transformation will be:**

Transformation of yourself, understanding your spiritual world, knows how to make dialogue with your soul (which you are), your mind (that is shaped by the exterior life mixed little with that spiritual tendency if you have nourished with your soul), with your heart (how it interprets feelings of thought and how much knowledge it has about feelings and how you feel healthy), your body (taking care of your body), understanding your purpose in this life, you are in harmony with yourself and will help others to be in harmony.

Life is art that take the shape of your eyesight, your eyesight is the sight of the soul, the sight of the soul is blurry by the influence of the heart and the mind because the heart and mind are trained by human rather than the influence of your real you.

**Food for your goal:**

1-love
2-eating healthy
3- having faith in your self
4-comonicating with your self
5- Spending time alone /daily/weekly/holiday.
6-Spending time where you love and feel good.
7- Spending time with people who you feel yourself.
8- Having your heart and mind open.
9-Treat yourself.
10- Tell others how you feel.
11- Remembering this is only and only your journey, your life.

*This list may change but for me right now that's what it is my soul food. What is yours?*

**Food for your goal**

# Stage 8
# Inspiration

Don't forget to pause and notice the amazing things and the blessings around you. This enables you to become inspired from anything that surrounds you, bad or good. You'll always have something to spark your inspiration and fire your creativity.

| Exercise | Answers |
|---|---|
| What does inspiration mean to you? | |
| Think about how inspiration helps your day to day life? | |
| Think about who does inspire you and why/how? | |
| Connect with nature what this mean? | |

# Exercise

Does nature help you focus and concentrate?

Does nature allow you to feel inspired?

Connect with babies what does it mean and feel?

Do babies inspire you and how/why?

Care about your needs…how do you do it and how would you like to do it?

Act and take what you need exercise created based on the individuals uniqueness.

# Exercise

# Answers

| Exercise | Answers |
|---|---|
| Care about your needs…how do you do it and how would you like to do it? | |
| Connect with people you admire….why and how? | |
| Do you shy away from people you admire or do you attempt to get to know them better? Why? | |
| Do you look at the good in others and try to make yourself a better person? | |
| Why is it important to have inspiration in daily life? | |
| What examples of inspiration can you think of? | |
| What inspires you daily and what do you get from it? | |

# Inspiration tree exercise

Fill up the tree exercise and soul food exercise.
I ask the individuals to create an exercise of what inspires they in the shape and order they prefer.

The inspiration stage is very unique and has to be personalised while working with individuals, groups or events energy.

- What does inspiration mean to you ? Why is it important for you to have inspiration in you daily life ?

- Discuss and then write your ideas on the board....
(Then amalgamate my views with theirs regarding inspiration).

- Mindfulness exercise ... connect with nature ... with babies. ... with people that you admire ... connect with your inner child, looking back to a time when you where happy.

| Notes |
| --- |
|  |
|  |
|  |
|  |
|  |
|  |
|  |

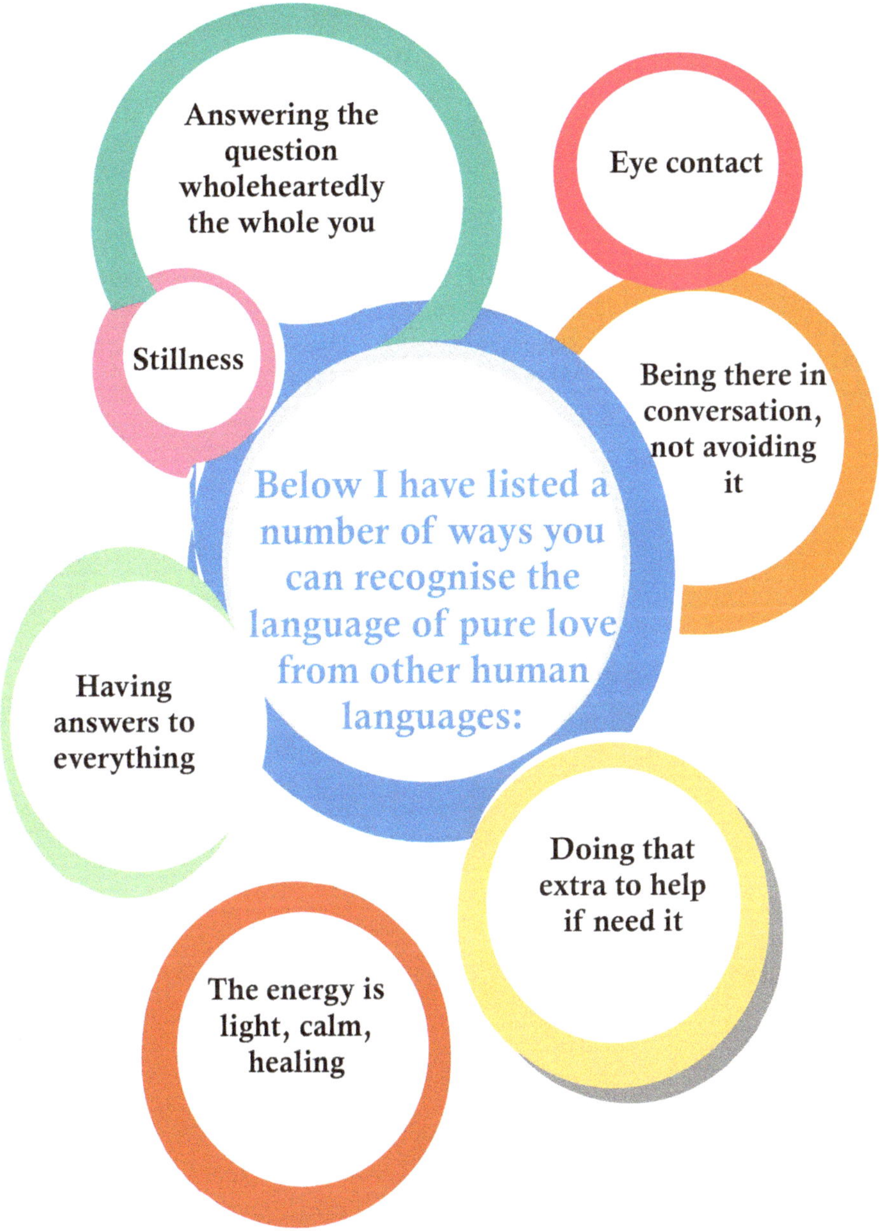

**Answering the question wholeheartedly the whole you**

**Eye contact**

**Stillness**

**Being there in conversation, not avoiding it**

Below I have listed a number of ways you can recognise the language of pure love from other human languages:

**Having answers to everything**

**Doing that extra to help if need it**

**The energy is light, calm, healing**

"The saying "open up your mind" does not resonate with me because the mind cannot be open, it cannot hear unheard words or things, it cannot see unseen things, it cannot learn from things that are not proven. Instead, I believe that the correct saying is "let your soul guide you". This means allowing your soul to be a part of your reality, a part of your decisions, of opening up to the universe and listening to new guidance, new signs, next stage of our journey ... to grow."

Our mind is just a robot that functions in a certain way, and the heart is the same. However, the body is something else due to the cells, as the cells feed in love energy. The body will remain healthy while operating on that food mostly, apart from when you abuse it physically by not looking after it effectively by eating, exercising, and fulfilling any other needs it may have.

Another reason the body gets ill is because of the path we have chosen before entering this journey. However, I do believe that every illness can be healed through pure love and guidance from your soul.

# Stage 9

# Commitment

Be a good listener and listen to your inner guidance, nature, and all your senses. Trust the universe. Give time and flow with time by being spontaneous in order to understand when the time is right to do what you need to do.

| Exercise | Answers |
|---|---|
| What does Commitment mean to you? | |
| What examples of your commitment are you willing to share? | |
| How is this example of commitment something other people can learn from? | |

| Exercise | Answers |
|---|---|
| | |
| Techniques and methods to stay committed: | |
| | |
| Have a goal in mind<br>Wake up with your goal in mind and go to sleep with the goal in mind | |
| | |
| Truly believe that it is a possible to achieve the goal you already gone through the stage of the goal | |
| | |
| | |
| | |
| | |
| | |
| | |

## Commitment exercise

Drawer Exercise - it involves organising your thoughts, goals, priorities, and responsibilities. We also need to be aware of the following; self love, purpose, food for the soul, karma, upholding your values and principles.

Life Ladder Exercise- You can replace the ladder with any object of your choice, however what is important it going through every steps of the ladder while also keeping in mind the 80% and 20% we talked about regarding self love.

Through this exercise you will find yourself where pure love is, there is the vision of your life that you have to choose and turn into reality. Every step of the ladder should feel right for you, and once you come to practice the first step below you can get better understanding of the other steps. Therefore, it is important practice the first step in which you get to talk with the silence and the energy that is explained in the first step below. This will help you to complete the ladder excise after understanding the steps below.

# Drawer exercise

# Stage 10
# Affirmation

Tell yourself how good you are. Remind yourself of all the amazing things you are doing and the great abilities you have to help you fulfil your purpose.

| Exercise | Answers |
|---|---|
| What are affirmations? | |
| These are ways we: | |
| Support | |
| Discipline | |
| Guide ourselves to achieve our tasks | |
| | |
| | |
| | |

| Exercise | Answers |
|---|---|
| How do you use them? | |
| Do you discipline yourself when necessary? | |
| Do you offer yourself emotional support? | |
| How do we create Affirmation? | |
| Do you have a goal in mind that you wish to achieve? | |
| Do you have the necessary structure in place for you to succeed? | |
| | |
| | |
| | |

# Exercise

## Answers

| | |
|---|---|
| Who decides when we need them? | |
| We decide when we need them, when is that and why? | |
| We decide what type of affirmation works for us | |
| When we use them and how we use them? | |
| We use them when we feel that we need to change something about ourselves. | |
| We use them as reminders to make us stay on the path we want. | |
| | |
| | |

## The Affirmation stage work also involves co-working with the individuals.

- What are affirmations / How do you use them? (affirmation helps you to achieve what you want to achieve through reprogramming your mind, heart and body and finding the way to the real you? )

- How do we create them/why is important to create them? (only you know what is right for you and what works for you. Only you will know when to use them and how, however, you can start with what is provided in work book as a head start to your journey through magical module).

-Who decides when we need them/when we use them and how we use them? (Provide guidance on how to create affirmation as the individuals go along based on their journey through the stages of Magical module).

Conversations with yourself/soul/mind/heart/intuition and others. Remember the rules of the universe and that we should take 30 minutes out of our day for this and at least one day a week.

# Notes

One of the exercises to self inspire yourself and create your own affirmation from your journey is the program provided through the process of the magical module "HEAL YOUR PAST WHILE YOU WRITE YOUR BOOK".

The points below will be useful when going through the program. When you go through rereading it and structuring it, you will be surprised at what you wrote and of your abilities (refer to client 1 and 2 on chapter seven, who have started to write their books).

1-Someone to listen to you without judgment but with pure love.

2-Someone to give you advice as you write your free thoughts, automatically you will be connected to your inner child and your soul.

3-For someone to cry with and feel sympathy and empathy with you.

4-For someone you can discuss any confusions with.

5-For someone to laugh with at your stupidity and foolishness.

6-Someone to help you analyse and reflect on your mistakes/actions/experiences/painful moments/good memories etc.

7- After you finish the whole book you can decide if you want to help others with what you have created.

## More benefits that you get from this program are below:

Learn how to stay in the present, which can help you see things far more clearly.

Learn how to create a clear plan for the goals you wish to achieve.

Learn how to connect with your inner self; your true self.

Learn how to Connect With Your Highest Power.

Learn how to overcome the obstacles and to empower from them.

Learn how understand your role as a parent.

Learn how to love yourself in order to love others in the right way, enabling everyone to be happy.

Learn how to increase self-confidence.

Learn how to have more courage to approach things that you still do not trust, but that you want.

Learn how to Stay Realistic about your Desires and Reflect on what you really want.

Learn how to build cheerful and useful relationships, with yourself and others.

Learn how to heal yourself from your past.

Client one stated after her one-year work on magical module:
"The word meditation never really resonated with me but I never understood it and I did not know how to use it. But now I have found that what I do is similar but different, as it is a conversation with myself and it means mostly a conversation with the higher energy where I can contact my soul and the universe. Moreover I can have conversations with my soul, God, the universe and with my mind and heart."

My conclusion is that through personal experience and the work I have with my clients, conversations with yourself are very important if you know how to use it and guide the conversation. You must be guided by pure love in order to get the result you are supposed to or the result you're searching for. It is not productive co-sharing with yourself and the higher energy if you do not know how to do it and how to use it to make your dream life reality. You will know if you are doing it right once you realise that it is a solution for your suffering and begin finding pleasure in everything you do …through love you can see the magic in everything … you are in love with yourself, your life, and everything surrounding you, despite the reality that surrounds you, because the reality suits you and the things that you want … the energy that you give. It is important to understand pure love in order to have peace and harmony in your life.

For me to help the client in this direction I have to feel the energy of the person in connection with their higher energy and to understand the person as a human to help make the connection between the two and give the right guidance. Everyone is unique and different, everyone is in a different position on the journey of life, thus, everyone needs unique guidance which is personalised to their journey of life.

Below is an example of how I communicated through the connection of the soul with the client one. Having read one part of her book I created this post below and sent it to her through email.
"Whenever I read your writing, it seems like I'm in a boat in the water at light rain … and that's the energy of the universe or knowing what energy I'm up and running"

# Stage 11
# Love

Love yourself and everything on
this earth to attract the love
energy that leads to you living
in a magical world. Love is the
medicine of life and the place
where you get your answers

# Exercise

| Answers |
| --- |

What is love ?

Write two sentences on what you think love is

Then write another two sentences on why we love

How can we know we love ourselves fully?

By taking time to think to ourselves what do we gain and how?

By looking at ourselves in the mirror and see if you're happy about who is looking back.

# Exercise

How can we give the right love to others ?

By giving them the love we want to be given

By being a generally kind and good hearted person

How can we embrace the love of life?

Utilise the power nature gives us

Enjoy the little things about life

Be grateful for what you actually have that others don't and what does your soul tells you about this statement?

# Exercise

# Answers

Spending time in the place of love?

Being in nature helps you truly connect your body with your soul and allows your intuition to guide you

Create poem about love for yourself and life

Make a plan on how to keep your self-love

# Love

Love yourself, life, others, and everything that surrounds you ... this is the meaning of life ... this is the disappearance of dissatisfaction ... this is the disappearance of complaints ... this is the love without limitations .... free love ....magic love that creates magic on you and the life you are surrounded.

"The magic of life lies in your soul, where it finds the purity of pure love ... where there is only goodness ... where love is produced" (so whoever are religion leaders or people who represent themselves as good persons, you can feel it through the silence. ... the energy is in that moment ... "The sun can warm you up with the lights he has and you are not able to look at straight on with eyes because we are not pure as human .... is the same way when you look people on the eye ...you can tell so much about it if you just let the silence guide you").

I do believe everyone is unique and special.

We are not here in this world to be better the others but to be product of love and help those who has not achieved it yet to be product of love.

I discuss with clients the points below:

1- what is love, self love, universal love and imitate love

2- how each of it can be achieved

3- what are the benefits of it

4- how that can be practiced

5- what other research says about it

6- what religion says

7- why is it important what others say when has not been working?

8- connections we get with strangers ...like we know them for long time..... can see it through their eyes.

Is important to understand self-love, universal love and passionate/intimate love.

This life is for joy and the circle of life ....the generation is amazing and magical.

Your whole being is reaching toward greater understanding, greater Truth. Trust where your soul pulls you, it is into a more enlightened, aware state. Your friend is full of fear, but don't let his/her fear get to you. Your job is to remain calm and experience the Truth. Your soul knows the way forward.

We are truth seekers and never accept a teaching unless we have tried it out and find it to be true for us. I say never stop looking deeply, asking the questions, and testing it out on your own experience.

You can search throughout the entire universe for someone who is more deserving of your love and affection than you are yourself, and that person is not to be found anywhere. You yourself, as much as anybody in the entire universe deserve your love and affection." — Buddha

**Universal love is:**

Our body is build from love which will help us to function and that's why we have the need of others love, that's why we feel good around others but still there are things to reflect and think ... is it really satisfying us ? Or you just accepted because you think that is how far it can go ... for better !!!

Passionate/intimate love is on my understanding when two people are sharing their journey in all aspects of life and they don't need each other but they enjoy and love sharing their journey as they know themselves and they are sure of each other. There are two klient who have achieved pure love on self-love and they know how to share love in universal way and they are ready to get in intimate, passionate love, as they are clear of what they want. This love will last happy after forever.

175

Each points below are the base of pure love:

1- Treat others the way you like to be treated
2- Love your self the way you like to be loved
3- Do your best in everything you decide to do

 ### Treat others the way you like to be treated:

-In order to know what is best for others first you have to know what is good for you and for that reason you have to have self-love to know yourself well and to feel loved in order to help others on their needs.

People who have self love they know the answer to this question but for those who don't have self love you have to raise your awareness on those points below before you get involved on with others or interact with others as you will end up hurting yourself and others:

Before you process the though its on your head consider how is helping the other? How do I know it's really helping the other? What is the length time my help will last and what they will do after that? What is costing me to help others? Can I find a way that can help them to help themselves in long term? If I was on their place what I really wanted? And take deep breath before getting the answer or best is before you ask the question to yourself as it allows you to connect to your true self and listen to the true answer instead of the ego answer. In my understanding from my self-discovery the ego is the mind created based on thoughts that takes us easy options and just thinks for themselves and never consider the other best interest. The true self is the soul, the pure energy link directly to creator and that is all about helping you to be pure to yourself, which that leads automatically to be pure to others.
The ego, the part of mind that is fulfilled with information and guidance how to gain things (things such as , money, love , affection, attention, fame, life style to show off ect)only for your self that is not pure because you will hurt others for your interest, such us lie, manipulate, physically hurt others, steal, emotionally hurt others and lots more that you may think off or seen around.

If you manage to see the difference between the pure thought and ego thought than you have started the first step of practising on treating others the way you like to be treated. Remember if you have not achieved the self love then you will not know how to treat yourself and you are lost on ego which you notice as you don't feel fulfilled, loved and complete exactly where you are and you need help before you start to help others or think you can help others as you are effected by your ego and need healing through your soul.

The self-love will help you to link to your purest side, which is your soul and then you will treat yourself with pure compassion and understanding and you will know how to treat others.

### 2  Love yourself the way you want to be loved:

We never learnt how to love ourselves because growing up we have always been told that we shouldn't be selfish and only think about ourselves. I truly believe that this was both a misconception and misunderstanding as we failed to value just how unique children are. I think both people and culture in general have both misunderstood and failed to value children for the special beings they are. We can undeniably learn from the children about self love guidance or those three rules I mentioned earlier, as they can give explanations as they are pure. They are also under the influence of their soul. Around the ages of 3 and 5 and then around the age 7 the children tend to be very connected to the creator, then depending on the amount of compassion and understanding they have received by people that surround, they will begin to be defined. This happens up until the age of 16, and by 19 years old you finally build a strong connection to the creator and your soul. Up to the age of 25 years individuals work on shaping themselves and choosing which way to go... do they follow their ego or their soul? As mentioned earlier, many people ignore the soul and they do not follow that route (as statistics show about crimes, suicide, domestic abuse, depression, mental illness and generally unhappy people). It is challenging for young people between 16 and 25 to choose the soul route, as they fear the unknown. They struggle to accept their uniqueness and they don't want to stand out from others.

They choose to follow the same path that others have followed, in order to be safe and conform. Others are part of the mind, the ego and often these individuals don't act in a pure way which consequently leads to pain, suffering, unhappiness, wrongdoings and pretending to be happy (egoist).

Moreover, these individuals use their empathy skills to manipulate others  in order to get love and satisfy their needs. The ego exists within all adults, however egoism in children does not exist. Consequently, adults teach children that they should not be egotistical or act in a way which may be perceived as egoist. By doing this, the adults have repressed the children's desires to continue being pure and unique. I discovered self-love through asking demanding questions to both the creator and nature around the age of seven. I refused to be defined by my ego or the mind, beliefs and opinions of people who surround me. By rejecting unhappiness, I managed to gain self love. I had developed self love which in turn intensified my self belief. I now believed that I could make my dreams a reality, which I eventually did by ending up where I am now. In simple terms, you must push yourself to discover the pure love buried deep inside you, in order to develop self love through compassion and understanding as you are guided by your inner pure love. Once you have figured that out, you'll finally understand the importance of time and money and know how to manage it in order to balance your inner world with your outer world.  It is very important to know a simple fact; we are born, we die but the soul does not die. A fact which have been proven by science. So for that reason a creator does exist, he has created the circle which I explained on the stage of acceptance and in the literature review about the law of the universe.

The law of the universe is simple, you simply need to be pure and want justice for yourself and others. You have to show compassion, understanding, care and love towards you as a whole and others as a whole. That is the law of the creator that leads to fulfilment, peace and being loved.  If you lose your way then you will be unhappy, not in peace and not loved until you learn to find the way to be who you truly are.

178

The creator has created pure babies and there are no babies who are not pure. Your responsibility during this journey is not letting your heart or your mind interfere in the pure baby. I truly believe that our life journey depends on our previous achievements and circumstances. That's why I strongly believe that achieving self-love will help you to feel fulfilled, happy, in peace and loved. Once you have achieved that you will see things differently, you will see people differently, you will see life for what life is, you will create magic sparks through your creativity and curiosity. You will spread pure love whatever you go. Remember that anything you do that is not a part of genuine pure love, compassion, justice and honesty with yourself and with others, is not part of gaining self-love.

It is very simple to love yourself. It takes willingness, determination and a strong desire for pure love and care for yourself. This will enable you to connect with your soul, which is the purest part of you as an individual and is a part of the creator. But to connect with your soul you have to be demanding and set on working on yourself to discover how to want justice and love from your self to your self. That can be done through the stages of the magical module, which combines numerous techniques with creative inner conversations guided by you.

## Loving yourself:

1.  Learn to accept and love yourself for who you are and the way you are. Analyse what you do not like about yourself and plan how you're going to change or make improvements. Alternatively, you can accept these flaws and not complain about them.

An individual who wants to be loved does not waste time on overthinking, complaining, moaning, wanting what others have, not liking their image, wanting others to love them, judging others, talking about others when it does not benefit the person they are talking about, wanting more money , etc.

Accepting yourself means allowing yourself to show compassion and understanding towards the person you are and having deep conversations with yourself in order to discover who you want to be. You need to go through the stages of momentum and acceptance in order to completely understand this point and ultimately achieve it.

2. What we give energy to, that is what we attract. If you focus your energy on all your problems then those problems will follow you. Alternatively, if you focus your energy on finding solutions then these solutions will become a part of you. When seeking a solutions, quietly step back in order to view the whole the situation, the problem or the issue that is presented as a whole picture. We have to show compassion and consideration to the whole of us before we decide on a solution. Refer to the goal stage for more details.

3. Let go of the things that hold you back from being yourself. Once you start to be a product of justice towards yourself and others, it is difficult for you to stay around those who don't practice the same justice towards themselves and others. This is because you want to be truthful and being truthful requires lots of energy and skills, in order to learn when and how to be honest without hurting others. Until you learn how to be truthful and you practice justice you must keep your distance from those who complicate your journey or become obstacles.

4. Be aware of all the negative obstacles but focus on the goal. Be aware of the fear that you are feeling. Talk to the fear so that you can understand it and reassure it that you have a plan.
It is through your inner conversations that you can make the following points happen:

Turn pain into compassion and understanding.

Turn fear into a plan, as you become more aware of what your fear is telling you.

Turn anxiety into self belief.

Turn loneliness into the comfort of your pure love and dance through your pure love.

Allow your soul to be a healer of your mind and heart through your inner discussions.

**5** Ensure that you are clear about your visions in life and frequently revisit them. Make sure that you live 100% in the present, so that you can fully enjoy everything you do in the moment. This involves being 80% productive at what you do in the present and 5% revisiting the past if you require any lessens or any good memories. Furthermore, the remaining 15% is dedicated to future visions and to moving forward to get to where you want to be.

**6** Dream big, visualise your dreams, and break them in small goals. Loving yourself is the most amazing thing that I have discovered and it is something which has helped my clients be content, appreciate what they have, learn to feel loved within, know with who to share universal love, know which kind of partner they want , how to treat others through compassion and understanding, planning for their goals, making time for themselves, noticing the little things that make them happy, valuing themselves, believing in their abilities, understanding what others say and do, and smiling to themselves in the mirror and to the world.

**7** Your intuition and your soul provide you with guidance. Ensure that you find time to listen and have conversations daily. Don't just start a conversation and then simply ignore it because it is deep and needs more energy, attention, focus, will, determination, creativity on questions asked, curiosity of seeing

181

things in all areas that can benefit you and your life journey, including others involved, ensure you reach the end of the conversation with you eventually come to a conclusion, plan and out it into action.

**8** Pursue your passion and find a job you love and enjoy so that you give your best. Through those inner conversations, you have to discover the ways you can pursue your passion and enjoy the job you have decided to do. Remember we have one life which we need to enjoy and make the most. Have those inner conversations daily and as often as you need. End these conversations with reflections, analysis and actions?

**9** Consistently surround yourself with things that are meaningful to you.

Know who to socialise with, as you are meant to share universal love. Those who have not discovered self love are unable to share love, instead they will just feed on your self love. You should be aware of this and make decisions accordingly.

Ensure you have a purpose regardless of how you choose to spend your time. Your time is the key to your peace, love and creating the reality you want and enjoying the moment.

Have daily inner conversations in order to evaluate how your day went and reflect on what you did, what you wanted to do or what you could have done.

**10** Ensure that you live your life only for yourself and no one else; it is yours and only you can decide how to live it. Every time you feel like something is not going the way you want, you have to stop all the thoughts, all the emotions and just connect with your higher power, with your soul, your creator and see everything from their point of view. You will understand why you are important and why it is important to make yourself satisfied from a pure love point of view and not an ego point of view. Your achievement of pure love cannot benefit other, unless you help them achieve it from within. We are here to help ourselves, not to rely on others. Of course others can help us move forward and climb our steps a bit faster, but that's it. So help which does not help the individual to help themselves in not beneficial, except for when you know that your help is helping them to progress two or three steps forward. This is why it is important to focus on being content, without relying on others. It is only when you are content that you can help others in the correct way.

11 Believe in your uniqueness and the universe will guide you. Remember if you can't accept and love yourself just the way you are you will not have confidence, high self esteem, lots of doubts and not sure that you deserve what your vision is. Easy could be alloying yourself to feel for those who keep buttering you. So you need to have a serious conversation with your soul to find ways how to feel loved and to remind yourself all the good things you have and those that you are in progress to get. Continue to reflect on your progress of the changes that you have decided to make. It's important to find ways how to feel loved through your pure love in order to shine and enjoy everything you do and you will recognize the truth from the lie, the compliment from someone who is trying to make you like them. Use of manipulation for their interest only, you will know someone who has problem with themselves but instead they put you down, you will appreciate the critics, the truth, genuinely and straightforward people.

12 Treat everyone the way you like to be treated, to receive the same from the universe. This is very important and need lots of awareness, attention, and reflection from the soul and creator point of view. Also needs healing time for your mind and heart after each

situation that did not feel right to you. Healing can be done through your soul by allowing your soul to be the therapist for your thoughts and feelings. Moreover reflect daily through your inner conversations on how you have dealt with others from whole you but the soul and creator has to have the last say if you trust your soul and the creator. Sometimes we follow their guidance even without being clear or making sense but later we will understand.

When you start the journey through the self love can cure all emotional and physical illness as you will become product of pure love. You will only be part of pure love, no judgment, no anger, no getting upset more then what is need it for healing time, don't hate anyone or anything, you will allow understand of others and show compassion. You will feel loved , never feel lonely, you will know your value and you will not accept less then what you deserve. You feel confident, strong, you will have the highest intelligence as you get information directly from the soul which knows everything and creator. You will not relay anymore on your mind and heart because your awareness has improved on observing your thoughts and feelings though the healing sessions from your soul. You can see through others and understand their actions instead of judging or getting angry as you know the ways how to get what you want in the way that is recognized by universe and others as is the language of love.

##  Do your best in everything you decide to do:

Doing your best means working hard to discover and achieve self love, which is the key to fulfilment, peace and love. Self-discovery sets the foundations for an enjoyable life in which you are fulfilling the purpose of your existence. A number of the qualities include: - create - Analyze options - choose the options – look for justice - love - diplomacy - sharp observation - work- simplicity - wish - plan - a short and long vision for the future - dedication - reflection - decisions - purpose - and the magic of love is to love yourself and you life, the way you want to and not how others impose.

# The ingredients of knowing if you are doing your best are:

Cry if you need to cry but get find a solution and move on

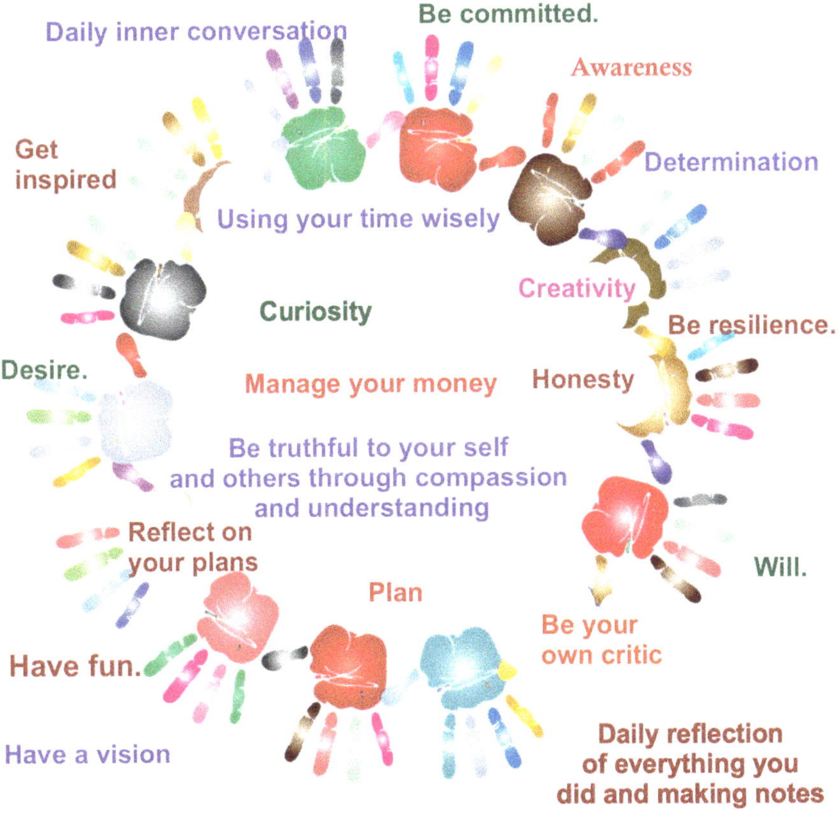

Be committed.

Daily inner conversation

Awareness

Get inspired

Determination

Using your time wisely

Creativity

Curiosity

Be resilience.

Desire.

Manage your money     Honesty

Be truthful to your self
and others through compassion
and understanding

Reflect on
your plans

Will.

Plan

Have fun.

Be your
own critic

Have a vision

Daily reflection
of everything you
did and making notes

185

Reflect/evaluate
your thoughts and feelings

Reflect on your actions

Put
yourself first

Be best friends
with the creator

Focus on your
goal and purpose

Demand that you are a product
of justice towards yourself
and ask the creator
to get what you need.

Write down your plans, ideas,
steps and anything
that is new to you and you
think is useful to you.

Never rely on others.

Finish your
inner
conversation
until you
come to a
conclusion
and a
decision.

Ask for what you need
to know and create
ways to help you find
the answers, during
your inner
conversations with
your soul and creator.

Be an active listener
to your inner
voice and to the
creator/universe

Show compassion to your self

Keep true friends whom
you value and who speak their minds.

186

Look after you body, mind and heart through your soul guidance.

Ask for help when you think you need it.

Search for the people who are on the same journey and be aware of your inner guidance while you're reading, listening or watching what they are saying.

Be aware of the opportunities.

Trust but be aware of not trusting and as soon as you see signs of doubt, keep it in back of your mind until you can prove it.

Get inspired daily by small meaningful things.

Believe that everything happens for a reason, thus you have to discover it or just keep going if it feels right.

Only trust your soul and creator.

Accept the unknown and develop the right skills to learn how to deal with it. The unknown is a part of our journey and the beauty of life.

Say sorry when you know that you are in the wrong.

Analysis of the options you have.

Appreciate what you have and have a clear vision of what you want and how to get it in small steps.

Raise awareness of time length between each step of the plan and leave room for flexibility.

187

# Stage 12

**Practising three main life guidance in order
to keep the balance of self-love......
test to be taken at this stage**

*For each points below to be given scenario as exercise
and discuss it afterwards....*

*Treat others the way you
like to be treated*

*Love yourself the way
you like to be loved*

*Do 100% in everything
you chose to do*

Daily how you can practice those three rules on your daily
experience?  Give an example of the worse day and of a good day
you had.

| Notes |
|---|
|  |
|  |

**Appreciation of what you are and who you are**

Kindness

To love yourself and the other

Imagination

Inspiration

Reflection

Analysis

Planning

Create

Passion

Justice

Love without any interest just love

Looking for solutions

Decisions based on the goodness of justice to oneself and others

Conversation with yourself / argument / discussion / disagreement / decision / sense / acceptance / inspiration / love

The main ingredients of purity: Show demonstration of ingredients applying to your days you mentioned early on in previous exercise.

Want to achieve the things you want to achieve since you were a child even though you think are impossible. …. do detailed plan and achieve. ..work

Planning

Dedication

Working

Searching

189

**Recap of everything and discuss ways how to maintain the balance from what you have learned so far ....**

# Exercise life map since you remember and up to now :

## Up to here in total time scale is one year

# Just thoughts of moment on how I have started connecting with my true self:

✻ Through eyes of my parents specially my mum

✻ Through anger at age of 7 to get answers from creator and nature including talking to animals

✻ Then after age of 7 up to age of 18 th I did not need it as I just did it through enjoying life adventure. ...I was fullfilled and content

✻ Around age 18th to 22 I done it through communicating with my best friend. ..

✻ Around age 23rd to 36 I done it through speaking to strangers, seeking love from others, reflection of my own vision of when I was 7 years old and 18th

✻ Then 36 up to 41 I done it through spending time with myself. ...and when I was with others I need it wine in order not to be drown into their energy but be me still......

✻ Now at age of 42 I don't need drink anymore to be me around others as I grown and I can be me fully by practising my own techniques explained on my books
or my map life below:

# Stage 13

Practice and keep the balance of self-love in every day and everything you do .... Master of magical module and three main life guidance we mentioned earlier on, stage 12.

At this stage will be need it to evaluate their practice after one months they have finished stage 12 to see how they have got on. Will be provided unique exercises disegned based on their life style.

# Stage 14

**Keep the balance of harmony of peace and love with themselves, others and life . …. managing higher energy ….. the harmony of the soul**

"Life is Magical ….You are Magical " is a education book and self help book to reach fulfilment/contentment and feel love in present moment not waiting for tomorrow …..We have it as option to discuss chapter 7, 8, 9, 2, 11 in order to evaluate their balance of life. Where they are with the energy level and which strategies they are creating in order to continue living in peace and love they already have created up to this stage working through MM.

*Furthermore may create few exercises based on what you bring at this stage to help you grow further.*

Attachments in my opinion is not healthy as is not produced by pure love but by mind and heart from the information we grown in outside world. .... and we operate from outside to inside when we use attachments. ...

But when we use pure love instead we operate from inside to outside world.

Your desire to learn to love yourself must be greater than your desire to protect yourself from pain, rejection, grief and anything else you fear..


"An individual who gain self-love will not be abused in any form and will not abuse anyone......because self-love leads to being guided by their soul (that is pure love) and being able to listen to their intuition (voice of creator) Can get guidance how to handle situation in their best ways and protect themselves from anything danger "

Also the question is .....how do you help children who are going through suffering to turn into self-love and Heal themselves? ...Imagine when is harder to do that with children that already they have love within and they do shine through but they don't recognise it ....imagine how hard is to help adults to achieve self-love. ....

Remember self-love is the key to fulfilment /contentment and feeling loved. ...to enjoying fully life. ..

And the world is not in peace and love just because people have not achieved self-love. ...we have not been educated to have self-love. ... Even the meaning of self-love is very few people who know and very few who know how to apply it in practice. ....

"Of course through darkness you want light"
" Most of people who don't go through darkness they don't even question if is light but they just stay in same level ....those who goes through darkness they get drown by darkness or they search for light "

This advice goes only for people who are guided by mind and heart but not those people who are guided by soul ....... because this advice will be replaced with this one below for people who are guided by soul

"Just say what you think at the moment as long as is understood in the way that benefits you and the other. Angry, happy , sad are just what you getting from others and need your understanding, only with breath can help understand the harmony so it allows you to do the best for you and the other "

Momentum > get to communicate with your soul, get in touch with your true self , with purity that you have been born with , understand your mind and your heart ....alloy your soul to organise your thoughts and Heal your heart.

Acceptance > is about accepting the whole process in momentum stage and the reality is surrounding you .....use the process in momentum stage to understand your reality and accepted. Raise your awareness of what you want to change and how you will get it ....

So this stage you start to be fulfilled if you have started to practice the momentum stage to practice purity so it alloys you to connect with your true self (soul ) and through the soul you see clear your thoughts in your mind which need to get organised and the feelings in your heart that need to be healed. ....

If you have not done the momentum stage properly can not swim to other stages being fulfilled/content and feeling loved. ......

196

Other stages are goal, inspiration, commitment, affirmation and love

You want to be happy, fulfilled, content and feeling loved then practice purity in order to get to know your own soul ......and just alloy your soul to guide you not your mind or heart .....Through your soul you get to hear clear the voice of creator (universe )

Power for me is when it comes from individual practising purity and have clear vision how the life journey wanted to be .... and that power is all you need to be fullfilled, content NOW and get the reality you want......

For me that is power and success. ....

Enjoying each moment of life ....

Our power does not come from outside world. ...because the power comes from outside world is not pure and definitely will not make you fullfilled, content and became pure love the way we have been born. ..the way the babies and children under three are ...the way children up to age 25 are more under influence of pure love (soul ) then adults. ...

So we have the power within and just need to keep feeding it by practising purity in order to spread power in outside world. ...

# Stage 15

Master self-love, work on practicing how to help others around you……explore your passion into contributing into the world

2.How can we make people believe that happiness is here and now in whatever we choose to do? And is not in the material world……

6.How an adult can be a child ….as children are happy most of the times ..... but using the adults power?

1.How to make people to love themselves, others and life ?

Self love master:

exercise to stimulate your self in deeper level of life philosophy

5.How can we enjoy working on what we want to achieve?

4.How the child who is with bad parents can still love themselves and life?

3.How can someone who eats only once a day and dont have house to sleep can be happy and love themselves and life?

7. What advice you give to adults to be happy here and now and achieve their dreams…..?

**Example of someone's answers:**

1- loving yourself is a process, because often people confuse loving yourself with narcissi's, or selfishness... loving yourself is a hard work to be pursued but is the only way towards permanent happiness

2- loving yourself ....is an idea that people misunderstand and confuses with the love for outside world.... material things...

3 They say you appreciate things that you don't have anymore....as results you look beyond your view .. what a homeless wants is basic and consequently they feel essence of life ...

4 depends on the circumstances and the purpose, the model that the child will take in life ...
5 we can enjoy the work if we go through the hardship and see achievement where we thought is not possible... success without difficult roads does not exist ...

6-Without gaining self-love is not possible to be happy because you will be swimming in confused roads that don't bring you home.....you will not feel home

7- is not about to make a difference, but it must be conscious that it passes through difficult paths that can end happy ... Life is one and living with personalized or idealized forms (people we have modelled) Not always true or correct believe that you are just and you and your works others can be simply small particles because people live in community...

The subconscious accounts for at least 90% of our thoughts, emotions and behaviours and by definition, is the part of our belief system that we are unaware of. Learn how to muscle test with this video instructional and how to use this powerful tool to communicate with your body, subconscious and soul.

# The pure energy is our soul: how we work with energy?

Energy is created by everything ......by our inner world and outside world... explain the energy created by our inner world and outside world.....how we can notice the difference and how we can directed towards purity ?

200

The Energy is the direction of our vision…..and we are the master of the energy…..how you understand it, how you are playing the role of the master of the energy, give me example of how your energy is directing you towards your vision or other way around….because if you are not aware of your energy then the energy is taking control of your life….

If we have unclear things …..is important to stay in that energy until we clarify and understand what is happening ….is like a depression state ….but with limit of time and aim to come to solution ….to come into light ….to shift the unclean energy to a clean energy ……this can be done through stages of MM to go through for each confusion that we have …….

**Momentum:** stay in that energy until we understanding it where is causing it and what can be the action plan towards the solutions……if we feel to be sad ….we must alloy our self to explore all the emotions and thoughts we are having…… give me an example when you have done something similar …..and describe the process you have done it, including the outcome you got …..

**Acceptance:** To accept all our feelings and thoughts that are going through us …..one by one and through our pure love give them the right support ….. in order to serve our peace, love and future plans …… give me an example when you have done something similar …..and describe the process you have done it, including the outcome you got …..

**Goal:** After you passed the first two stages of MM then you get used to the goal and action plan you choose it …..embrace it ….as it is not easy to reprogram your thoughts and heal your emotions link to the situation you are experiencing ……it needs some qualities to keep going and move on towards your aims and goals….. give me an example when you have done something similar …..and describe the process you have done it including the outcome you got …..

Inspiration: this is the stage where you need to find your unique inspiration to have courage and to remind yourself the qualities you have and to love your "why" ....why you want what you want to achieve ........ give me an example when you have done something similar .....and describe the process you have done it including the outcome you got .....

Commitment: is about staying in the higher energy and finding ways and strategies how to keep disciplining yourself.... Discipline means practicing self-love ingredients. Give me an example when you have done something similar .....and describe the process you have done it including the outcome you got .....

Affirmation: Affirmation is to help you be creative and create new personalised affirmation about yourself and link to the situation you are handling.....also can use the previous affirmation .......lets create 3 affirmation link to your exercise you done today ....

Love: This stage is to give love to yourself , remind yourself how much you appreciate yourself and what you want to do ....including what you have .....write down 5 qualities each sentence that I explained .....

This process has to have time limit and can't be more then three months as it goes to unhealthy depression ......but through practice can be minimised to few hours process .......or few minutes while you having a walk, a coffee, or a chat with a good friend, or listening to music, or having a drink alone, or having a relaxed bath....ect that's the way you can shift the lower energy of the mind, heart, body to your higher energy....

This technique can be done for any problem/challenge/emotional disturbance/confusion/ etc ....

Unblock your body's energy and let in an abundance of wealth, love, vitality, and meaning to your life.

Lets do exercise on the meaning of the words below link to the example you can bring and how you apply it through purity:

Perfection

Brain food

Balances

Light

Viewing the mirror

The noise of the mind

Control of emotions

Silence returned to wish for wealth

Suffering.....
the inspiration to be done better than those that cause suffering - shamelessly frustrated turned into anger

Reflection of the mirror of love with curiosity and amazement.....
but with pleasure pursuit of absurdity ... feeling unmanaged but feeling right

Supressed pain turned
into competition
achievement

The fear of turning
in an strong mountains

No judgment in the
simplicity of love.....
shining of light

An old soul in
the child .... ....
as it is clearly is
noticed

Kids grow... it will come time when they will be in road crossing where they have to decide which way to go ....we only can be behind them when they fall or when they need reminding how good they are

Love is the greatest force in the Universe. It is higher intelligence. We have a choice to create consciously, to learn and expand our understanding of what Love means, how to align with Love and how to allow ourselves the experience of Love.

We are Love already. The more we interact, the more of the Light and Love we bring into ourselves. This is how we transcend what locks us away from our full Love expression. Each of us is Love already and each of us will experience this journey towards our

Loving Self in a different and a very unique way. Each of us is transcending different aspects of ourselves, different limitations but also opening to different gifts, talents and new aspects of ourselves.

When we open towards more Love and loving relationships, those naturally enhance our gifts and abilities. They help us to grow into the best of us and who we are.

If this resonates with you, let's be more Love.

Ever since I learnt to be a product of pure love, my life became adventurous, fascinating, meaningful, peaceful, content, full of love and I was able to show compassion and care for others who were on my path. However, my literature review and others' quotes have shown me that I am not the only individual who discovered the solution to a peaceful life filled with love. I hope this book will help you to understand that happiness comes from an inner understanding of self-love and the ability to become a product of pure love. You are already a product of pure love deep inside, however, by following your mind and your heart you have failed to discover ways in which you can connect with your pure love that is your soul and to be guided by it.

Until you do that you will not be loved, feel peace, be content, fulfilled and able to love others in the right way. The right way is to want their best interest and let them explore what they want ... not using them for our own needs because we need them ... no we only need ourselves and once we become one with ourselves then we share the love with others ... we dance on universal love or passionate love instead of feeling hungry for their love. These are two different things; need of others and sharing love with others. If you have not achieved yourself love you cannot share love with others because you don't have love for yourself, you have not yet learned how to discover the pure love is within you and use it to give love first to yourself before you start to share as you need to learn how to keep producing love through your soul as we are using human parts and need to know how those parts function in order to spread love through our soul into all our human parts.

This is exactly what the stages of magical module help you to do but you need guidance from someone who has achieved self-love.

"If you propose to speak always ask yourself, is it true, is it necessary, is it kind." Buddha

"Peace comes from within. Do not seek it without". Buddha

"No one saves us but ourselves. No one can and no one may. We ourselves must walk the path. " Buddha

"To enjoy good health, to bring true happiness to one's family, to bring peace to all, one must first discipline and control one's own mind. If a man can control his mind he can find the way to Enlightenment, and all wisdom and virtue will naturally come to him." Buddhaa

"You, yourself, as much as anybody in the entire universe, deserve your love and affection. " Buddha

"All wrong-doing arises because of mind. If mind is transformed can wrong-doing remain? " Buddha

"We have freedom, we have been born to be have responsibility of our free will and free choices, we have choices, we are the one decide the decisions, life is free and only we can decide our life journeys, yes it is written but without our actions it can never happen and our actions can change our paths, our decisions are our responsibility that lead to take action that create the path " Vjollca Sadiku

"*Holistic Spiritual Approach on Magical Module*"

VJOLLCA SADIKU
Co- Founder & Director
Magical Coaching

*Coaching Programe age 11 plus including individuals and groups (time scale is 3 months up to one year)*

# *Coaching Programe age 11 plus including individuals and groups (time scale is 3 months up to one year)*

What is Life Coaching? And how can it help you to create your own tools in order to achieve what you aim to achieve?

**Coaching Programme** is based on coaching qualifications and principles…completely different from the other programmes in this book. Each life coach has their unique way of delivering their training. My way is to start with deep questions in order to shake your balance completely so you can be able to observe your self from different point of view and then work on the topic you choose to work.

Life Coaches expose people to resources and information that they might not necessarily have had access it. And, coaches provide a source of motivation for helping people stay on track. We have the information but what we are lacking is the motivation to actually put that information to use. And that's another reason why people can reach higher levels of potential with coaches, and they can without them.

How does this benefit you? Well the answer is simple.
First off, there will always be a need for life coaches because people almost always need information that they are lacking in some capacity. Even if they have the right information, they will always need to be motivated.

This Coaching program consists of a step-by-step, easy to understand system that is going to enable you to understand and apply exactly what you need to help others take their life to the next level. Remember all my programmes have the healing energy on each word and are flexible based on what you represent…my creativity will be like an instrument of your life song combined with your life purpose and who you really are, who you want to be and what are you ready do to be who you want to be.

The menu of Coaching programme will be like a life menu activities:
Say hello, choose in menu…….and start with …..starters, main meal, desert, relax and start your journey…..

The menu of MM Coaching:

Say hello

starters

main meal

desert

relax

start your journey

# Momentum and Acceptance blended stage:

*Say hello activity:*
*The reason of this activity is to have a clear introduction and deep understanding of you and then let you chose in menu what you want for your treat or needs. (Time scale one month to delivery this stage with success)*

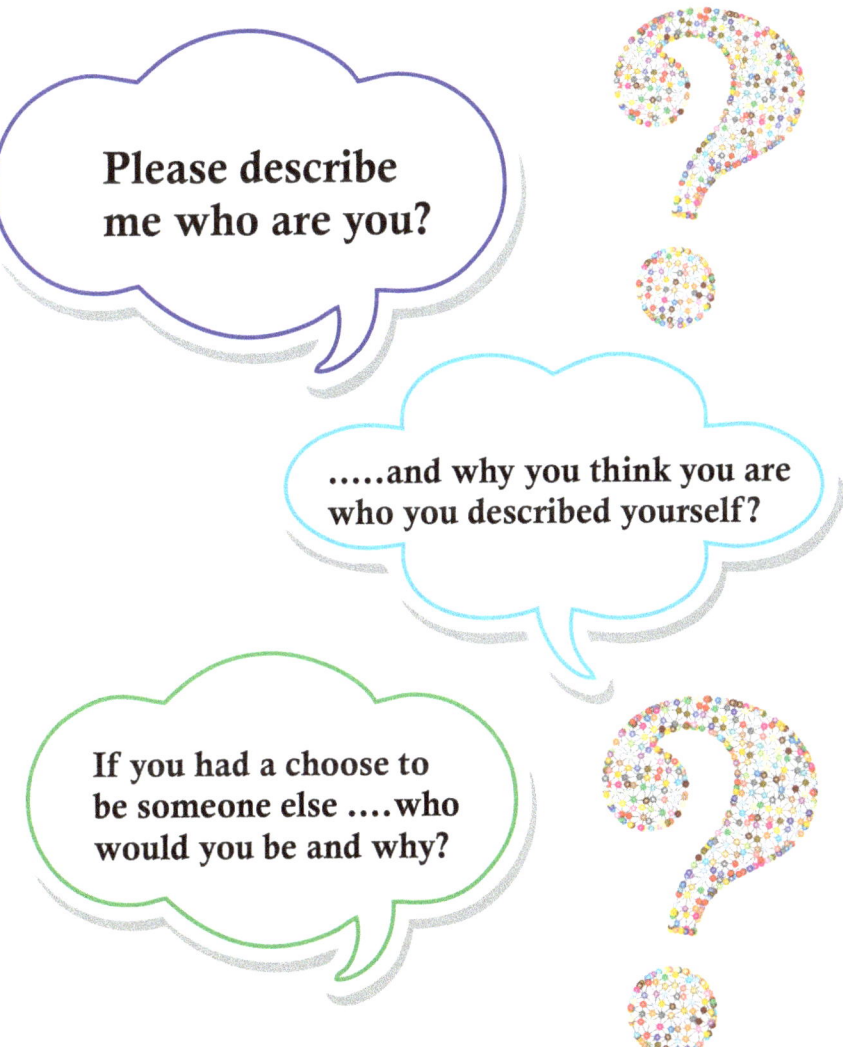

Please describe me who are you?

.....and why you think you are who you described yourself?

If you had a choose to be someone else ....who would you be and why?

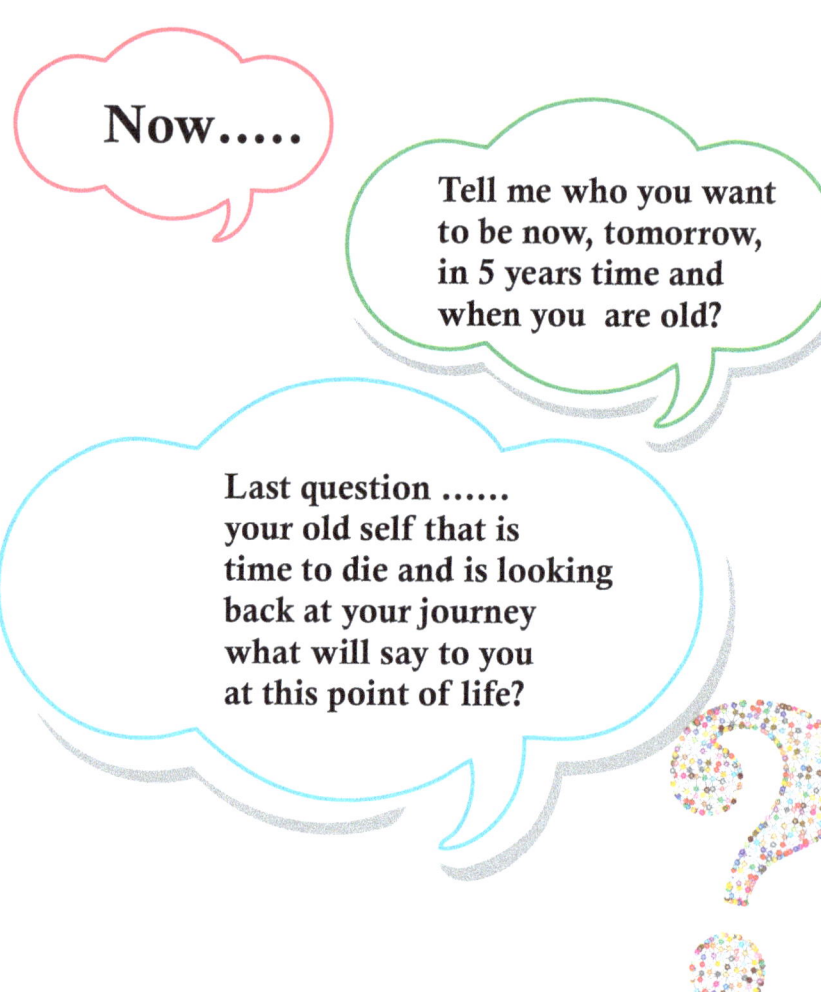

Now.....

Tell me who you want to be now, tomorrow, in 5 years time and when you are old?

Last question ......
your old self that is time to die and is looking back at your journey what will say to you at this point of life?

Reflection/discussion/conclusion write down and then you are ready to choose the menu.

It is important to understand your motivation to take action to make the goal into reality.

# Goal and inspiration stage of MM

**Choose in menu activity:** This will be designed based on the "Hello activity" but for now I will just do a general activity. Time scale is one month to be delivered with success.

You have to choose one goal and focus all your energy on working at that goal as it may have five or seven sub goals that need to be explored and put them into action plan......Also can choose three or five goals and work on surface of each goal to create action plan.

Each option will have followed up homework; feedback, reflection, discussion and action plan how to keep moving forward on self-help guidance.

After you choose the option has to be boosted the pure energy in option you choosing, need to know that you really want that option and you are 100% in love with that option.

Boost the love in your goal activity:

Lets focus on the future when you have achieved that goal and tell me what you see, what you feel, what you smell and describe what does it man to you at that moment when you have achieved that goal?

Do you still want that goal or you have changed your mind? (If you change you mind then I would recommend to work on the Holistic spiritual approach of Magical module programme (HSAOMMP) before you take coaching programme......or in self-love ingredients activity as part of the HSAOMMP.)

**Now …..**

Put your goals in order. Take your top 10 goals. These are the
ones that you are going to work on first.

 Define your goals and pot them into drawers and put the
number on each drawer including your time scale to achieve them.

On-going goals needing daily input has to be specified and
describe in details the daily input is need it.

**Remember:**

Short-term goals could be achieved between one week and
three months based on the action plan you are designing.

Medium-term goals that may take between 6 months to a
year.

Long-term goals that may take longer than a year depending
on the journey of the goal blended with action plan you have
designed.

Feel up this tree with your shorter goals, medium goals and long term goals. Than in separate sheet you do each exercise for each of the goals.

# .......and start with .....starters:

## Starter activity: Time scale one months......

### Obstacles, Activity

We are going to explore everything that you want to do, including obstacles that may face or think you may face. This will assist you to set short, medium and long-term goals.

Please devote sample thinking time to each stage highlighted below.

### Stage 1

(This stages are to raise your awareness towards obstacles and to explore your inner power to overcome them)

Write down all the obstacles in detailed description by answering what are the obstacles? Why do you think they are obstacles? How would be with out those obstacles your life? How can you overcome them and what will you gain for overcoming obstacles? Why do you call obstacles and why you don't see it as steps to grow and get closer to achieving your goal?

### Stage 2

Write in one brief sentence why you want to overcome those obstacles on each goal on your list. If you can't do this with any of them, cross them off your list and create ways to create different journey to achieving your goals. Explore your imagination blended with reality.

Decide the most important areas of your life – for example…

Family

Friends

Career/ Work

Financial

Health & Vitality

Emotional well-being

Social life

Fun & recreation

Physical environment (where and how you are living and your surroundings)

Spiritual life

Add change or delete to include all the areas of life that are important to you. Define what success means to you in each of the life areas you have identified. How important is to you your inner peace and the feeling loved all the times? How can you keep the balance of your action plan to achieve your goal and other areas of your life?

## Stage 4

For each of your goals, ask if it is right and fair to everyone is my sphere of influence and concern and if it will take you closer to your overall objective. Explore and describe how you are doing the right thing by yourself and others involved in your life?

## Stage 5

For each of the goals on the list, expand your WHY. Explain to yourself fully why you want to have this goal and what it will mean to you. Write this down. (This is to boost your love for your goal in order to enjoy the journey of your action plan).

**Now you are ready for the main meal ......to take action towards what you decided to do and what you love to do.**


**Main meal activity:** Starting action .....time scale is one month to three month.


## Stage 1:

### Create action plan

Create a map for each goal in your list, put the order number and time scale next to each goal map you already have decided and make a list of tools you need for each step of the goal map road. Such as, people you need to work with or the people who can help you, the skills you might need to develop, what you need to measure and what you need to learn.

## Stage 2:

### Self-love activity

From the list below select the values that you feel are most important to you and explain why they are important to you. Also add any that are not included in this list. After you have chosen your values and had discussion of why they are important to you (it is important to have discussion in order to help you to be clear that those values are really important to you and you are sure they will serve you to be in peace and love here and now.... also we will discuss the definition of the list you choosed..and where those definitions has their roots) put them in order of importance.

219

Adventure    Art

Achievement              Challenge              Balance

Creativity    ?    Community              Nature

Democracy

Integrity              Time

Recognition    Health              Effectiveness

Fame

Patience

Helping others              Family              Honesty

?

?    Knowledge

Friendships              Awareness

Growth

Learning    Loyalty

Love              Laughter

Power

Order

Reward              Money

Religion    Pleasure

Responsibility    Relationships              Security    ?

?

Self-respect    Serenity              Status

Openness

Wisdom    Success              Connection

Spirituality    Stability    Truth

Spontaneity

Co-operation              ?

Understanding              Risk taking

**Then narrow down your list to the 10 most important values in order of importance.**

* 1
* 2
* 3
* 4
* 5
* 6
* 7
* 8
* 9
* 10

If you could only have one value for the rest of your life which would you pick and why? How is going to help you to be in peace and feeling loved here and now? How is going to support your action plan to achieve the list of your goals?

## Homework:

* 1- Keep daily diary of your action plans …..the work you going to do in the first step of each goal

* 2- Keep daily dairy of how your day went, how would you liked to be and what you going to do different for future

* 3- Keep diary what you want to talk to me about after one month we meet….or week ….depending on your progress of growth

# Commitment and love stage of MM

## Desert activity:

This stage and the last two could be delivered through self-help guidance also …..time scale for last three stages is between 3 months to one year……because is just a follow up work once a month or when is need it …..

This has to be part of keeping self-love balance ……and going through self love ingredients in page ….or going through what you are bringing link to the obstacles you are facing and go through the menu again in order to resolve anything that is blocking you from enjoying life here and now and working on your goals.

## Affirmation and love stage of MM

## Relax activity: Time with yourself/reflect/love/appreciate yourself, others and life

Keep a diary about all good things you are doing daily, what you have been enjoying, what you have done differently, what has given you mostly the pleasure, how you doing to fulfil your main purpose, how much time you had for yourself, 1 to 10 how fulfilled you feel and why, what has changed since we started to work together, what tools you have learned and what you have created, ……think how you are contributing to others and life around you. ………. this is link to affirmation and inspired stage of magical module.

# ...and start your journey.....

This stage can be covered by going through commitment and love stages of magical module in the HSAOMMP.

Furthermore answer questions below to understand your journey so far with the Coaching Program:

**2.How do you know that the answer of question one is right?**

**1.What have you gained from this programme?**

**4.What are your views for life now and how that has influence your future plans....?**

**3.What would you liked this journey to be different and why........or if you don't like nothing to be different .... why?**

**5.How might you s abotage yourself getting what you want?**

**6.How will you stop yourself from sabotaging getting what you want? Make a list of tools you have created to maintain your self-love and keep enjoying life while you work on your goals.**

**7.What have you done differently to share love with yourself, others and life? What advice would you give to those who don't enjoy life here and now all the times in any situation they may face?**

These tips below are for ages 11 to 16 years old:

## Writing exercises

sometimes writing things down helps us to express things we find difficult to verbalise. A youth/life coach might encourage their clients to write daily journals, write down how they feel or use charts, arts, and diagrams to identify their emotions.

## Games

light-hearted games and exercises help to build rapport and approach subjects and emotions that are too difficult to talk about in a focussed situation.

It is helpful for you to know how they can be contact in emergency situation because sometimes the deepest work is done on those times.

Using a great variety of methods, aim to inspire and motivate you and give you the confidence to realise your potentials and devise strategies for achieving your ambitions.

*"Holistic Spiritual Approach on Magical Module"*

VJOLLCA SADIKU
Co- Founder & Director
Magical Coaching

# 3 Mentoring programme

Mentoring Programme is to give you deep swim into the past in order to heal yourself from any blockage or pain that is stopping you to enjoy the present moment and have no limitation to your future vision. Then will bring to the present to explore the Magical Module (MM) stages and take you to the future in order to understand yourself, others and life. By understanding "you" will know the importance of self-love and work to gain your self-love of MM.....You will learn TO BE GUIDED BY YOUR TRUE SELF AND GAIN YOUR ABILITY TO LISTEN TO YOUR INTUITION ANYTIME YOU NEED GUIDANCE WHEN YOU ARE STUCK OR CONFUSED.

# Mentoring programme

Mentoring Programme is to give you deep swim into the past in order to heal yourself from any blockage or pain that is stopping you to enjoy the present moment and have no limitation to your future vision. Then will bring to the present to explore the Magical Module (MM) stages and take you to the future in order to understand yourself, others and life. By understanding "you" will know the importance of self-love and work to gain your self-love of MM.....You will learn TO BE GUIDED BY YOUR TRUE SELF AND GAIN YOUR ABILITY TO LISTEN TO YOUR INTUITION ANYTIME YOU NEED GUIDANCE WHEN YOU ARE STUCK OR CONFUSED.

A common emerging theme in the spirituality reflected by different religious perspectives, is the individual's or the group's attention on the inner resources and inner self. While many of us are aware that we have capabilities within that extend beyond the conscious reality, there are few of us, who sense them more significantly and/or are able to cultivate them by establishing an internal relationship, which results in a greater familiarity with this mystical phenomenon inside the self and its purpose in life. Those who chose and are able to engage with their inner world, discover that the resources in it are not immediately accessible, but become gradually noticeable by some kind of detachment from the external environment and/or regular spiritual practices such as meditation, and prayer (Dyson et al, 1997).

# Exercise to get into deep level of thinking.....
## the energy of your soul

Lets explore how we decide to come into this world?

What is the meaning of us being in this journey of life?

What are your unexplained experiences so far and how would you explain them?

What do you think about creator? ...how our world has been created and why?

What is intuition? Give few examples when intuition was speaking to you?

Who are you ? ....and why are you ......how would you define yourself now at this age , how would define "you" the younger self when you can revisit yourself at the younger age when you were very happy and anything you thought is possible ?....

Now try to have conversation with younger self about questions presented and write down conclusions of conversations and the answers of each question.

The spiritual world is the person you truly are (meaning: the soul).

The mind is simply a tool that carries all the information (taken from the time inside the mother's womb to the present point in the life journey you are). The mind has the ability to decide what information will be saved, etc. The heart produces feelings based on thoughts that arise from the mind. So, connecting a person with their soul has the ability to heal the mind and heart. That requires the individual looking after their mind and heart through the guidance of their soul, their true self.

Self- love is the key to everything and can be achieved by asking your self for justice, love and care towards yourself and others. Can be achieved through speeding time with yourself and having different conversations as longs as you consider those three main rules,

♡ 1-Love yourself the way you like to be loved,

♡ 2-Treat others the way you like to be treated and

♡ 3-Do you're best in everything that you do.

(How do you know you are doing your best? It comes through the inner conversations with your soul and your intuition). When you achieve to sharpen the practice of those three rules then you are able to love yourself and spread love around where is need it.

To achieve self-love you have to have those ingredients below and practice them daily in order to connect all the times with your soul and be able to listen to your intuition:

**Before we start the exercise below we will take few moments to regulate our breath in order to be in the right energy...the energy of purity....the soul in order for this exercise to give the result I want to get from it ......**

**Exercise stage 1 and stage 2 are based on the self - love ingredients:** asking your younger self to define each of the points below and tell you the reasons for defining it in the way they are defining……then lets share and discuss the outcome in order to come to the right definition here and now.

**Stage 2:** Take the final definition and describe in one sentence each how during your life journey that has served you, others and contributed to a peaceful and loving life?

**Exercise on exploring** and **defining universal** and **passionate love**, also revisiting your past in order to illustrate your answers. (This exercise is to help you know the important of **self-love** and to understand what has happening so far to your life journey is because you have not achieved self-love and you were searching for love in outside world).

## Universal love is:

Our body is build from love which will help us to function and that's why we have the need of others love, that's why we feel good around others but still there are things to reflect and think ... is it really satisfying us ? Or you just accepted because you think that is how far it can go ... for better !!!

Passionate/intimate love is on my understanding when two people are sharing their journey in all aspects of life and they don't need each other but they enjoy and love sharing their journey as they know themselves and they are sure of each other. This love will last happy after forever.

## Summary of the self-help process of MM:

How to connect with your soul: The summary of the magical module.

🌹1-Every day, spend a bit of time with yourself. Have a conversation with your inner peace. ... visit the time where you were a child. ... where dreams had no limits. .... where imagination stems from your dreams .... where you fly without realizing it you are doing it. .... where peace and love pamper you. .... where you have the courage to do anything. .... just to that feeling hold up and use that feeling to practice this exercise. ..... to continue and practice as long as you live in that feeling. ... then comes the second step down (but the ingredient must be based on purity, justice and goodness in every flap or imagination you create)

🌹2- Start the work with the mind. .... how? .... again with yourself, it begins in your silence and the feeling you gained from the first step, you can observe your mind through your soul with pure love and it cleans the thoughts you need and do not serve the feeling of the soul (love, justice ) and creates thoughts to help you achieve the reality you want. ..... this is a process in itself because every new thought should be accompanied by a detailed plan of

230

what you will do and how you will do it. ........ also with practice comes over time to create only thoughts that serve your soul. ... that feeling at the first step. .... always associated with justice, kindness and love. ..... that brings satisfaction, fullfillnes, mindfulness to your moments, peace, love and courage to create the reality your want....

3 - **Here begins work with the heart.** ....... here you need a very special care of your heart from your soul because ....... is sensitive and delicate. .... contradicts the thoughts but at the same time every thought creates a feeling. ..... If your thoughts are not protected by your pure love from other unjustness actions then it will create hurtful feelings ... so this process is longer than mind and difficult because there will be pain, tears, obedience with love and compassion of caring through your soul......... this process continues until all the every hurtful feeling is healed by the care of the soul. ......... and produces only feelings of pure love from the soul.

4- **Here we starts the process with the body**, then the common practice of all steps mentioned and keep practicing spending time with your self Getting to know you, how to keep up with your plans, how to find the right partner, how to love your self, how to be a good parent and how to do things today, not to regret yesterday or wait for tomorrow for things to happen because the present, here and now is everything that makes the difference and is important.

This process may take 3 to 5 years if you have the right holistic guidance and if you are determent to follow the magical module. Client one on chapter seven of the book "Life is Magical…You are Magical" has achieved it in one year because I was doing at least four hour each day holistic therapy and she was really determent to follow the three self-love teachings. The important is that since you decide to start and if you stay committed to the practice you will see the difference and feel your journey becoming fulfilling, peaceful, with love and meaningful. Remember it is an on-going process, as you can see in this example below, I have to be creative and curious all the times with my self and others or with every thing that surrounds us when something does not feel right.

# Swimming in past activity: Momentum, acceptance, inspiration stages of MM will be blended at this topic.

**My theory of impulses:**

🌻 **1- Mind impulses:** The Mind is a very important organ of our functioning as humans. If we use it under the guidance of our soul, it will take care of us and makes our journey easy because it is the computer that can store what we need to use in this reality. For example: if we don't look after our brain we will not be able to remember things and express ourselves through language. The brain and mind are the same word and are an important organ in order for our human parts to function physically and process the knowledge we get. This is when the impulse comes from your mind and is not associated with feelings or temptation but with calculated thinking. For example: you see a nice car, or nice house, or someone having money and nice life style, you have automatically think you should have it not them, that you should be in their place and even higher. If the impulse does not get processed by the soul then it will lead to shortcuts to get those things and your aims will be centred around it. There will not be time to think about who will be hurt or what are the consequences. The mind impulses comes from beliefs that are created to make the reality or how the reality should be from others perspectives, definitely not yours as you are not alloying your self to listen to you, to your soul and alloying your soul to make decisions, to do the reflection and analysis.

🌻 **2- Heart impulses:** The heart is very a precious organ, as we feel through the heart and it is responsible for every sensation we feel. It is a fascinating process but at the same time it is very dangerous if we don't take care of the heart through healing it, using our soul, as I explained in magical module. What do I mean by good feelings? For example if something really bad has happened, such as losing a loved one, or losing all the wealth you worked all your life for, or being disabled because of something that happens to you......how can we turn those feelings into good feeling? Well ....it starts with the momentum stage allowing yourself to feel and think

232

about what you are feeling and thinking through therapy or talking to family and friends. Then accepting what happened (again going through the stages of magical module it does help for any situation and any thing you straggling with). It means to accept that you are here in this life and the creator did not want you to finish this life journey yet for whatever reason that you have yet to discover. Yes, you do have a choice to end your life any time you want but you need to think through your inner thinking what you really want? If you want to end your life you are wrong if you think that pain will go away because will not as you have to start a different life journey exactly in that personal development that you have achieved it so far. But of course most of people don't know this and it can not be proven but if you ask your self deep down and stay with that silence you will know exactly what I am talking about. So the way forward is to love your pain because that will help you to find the light if you decide to search for light. You will not have reason not to search for the light. Like I said, the search for the light will automatically create good feelings. If you talking about the light as pure love and being the product of pure love, the search for pure love will help your heart to be healthy and feel good. Then you go through other stages of magical module to follow the search of pure love through that pain that you are experiencing. Impulses of the heart are very dangerous if they are coming from negative thoughts or thoughts that are not created in pure love within. Example: when you just want to be with someone even though you know that is not the person you can spend your life but you just want to satisfy your heart impulses. These impulses are so strong that it does not allow the mind to interfere. It Will just not listen to the mind because just want to satisfy the impulses. This definitely is not pure love and is not healthy for no one because you are hurting your self by being addicted to the wrong love and hurting the other person because you will end up arguing, fighting and not really loving each other. In this case again, you can heal your heart through inner conversation going through each impulses with compassion and understanding which will lead to help your heart see what is the best for your heart and what your heart really wants and how can it get it. The heart is place of love but need to make sure is place of pure love and not other feelings.

233

**3-Soul impulses:** In my understanding soul impulses are when you have to do something because you feel you are doing good and you are acting for the betterment of something. As impulses are based on pure love, which is you is your soul. But when you act on soul impulses you are exposed to danger and you are not fully protected by creator and your circle energy of your soul. That is because you are acting on impulses with out reflection and analysis which mean with not fully on decision that you have considered.

All the stages are blended with each other and are linked which means all the clients I took through a flexible journey based on my skills and what the clients provided at the moment. For details of each client journey and work has been done refer to chapter seven. This methodology that has been explained in chapter three could be as general self-guidance for the reader to achieve self-love. Similar guidance I have used for all participant on this research but not in order as it depends where the individual is and what is helpful and useful for at the moment.

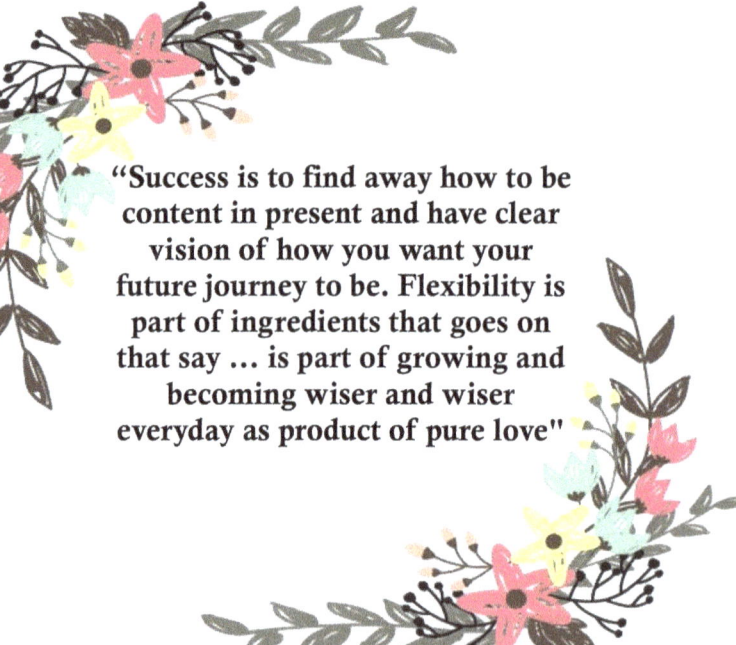

"Success is to find away how to be content in present and have clear vision of how you want your future journey to be. Flexibility is part of ingredients that goes on that say ... is part of growing and becoming wiser and wiser everyday as product of pure love"

**Creating magical healing experiences is in our inner power....we are born with tools to enjoy fully life and have the tools we need to create the reality we want.**

**What are some of the things my integrated HSAOMM do for you if you really want to work in deep level?**

1. It can help you overcome a stressful situation, relax, gain clarity and have more energy.

2. It may relieve physical, mental and emotional pain, accelerate natural healing, and prevent the progress of disease.

3. Dissolve grief, relationship conflicts and improve the quality of your life.

4. Detoxify the body's energy,, clear energy blockages, and release emotional baggage.

5. Unblock abundance blocks and gain the clarity to grow your business

6. Keep the balance of pure love here and now....in order to have the permanent inner happens that reflect on the reality you want and have.....

# Exercise on your understanding of impulses and your younger self .....how those definition are linked to your life journey so far and why ?

 1-    Write your own definition of impulses that we discussed early

 2-    Write few examples are impulses has influenced your life journey so far and what would you change about it or what learning you will take in order to create your inner peace and feeling loved within?

 3-    Now lets share and with each others therapist /guidance or help each other with minimum three things that we want to change based on the exercise we just did.

## Exercise to give energy to creativity:

Create one advice for each the statement below for yourself and someone that you know very well but use's those statements:

Imagine you are about to sit down/get up and tackle this task, right now....this task is not bringing you money at the moment , is just your passion and your inner voice telling you to do it because you love it and you know is for your own best and you have believe it will help others also .... But you have been facing with the thoughts below:

"I'm feeling a bit lazy; I'd rather just relax."

"I'm so busy, how can I squeeze in the time?"

"Why should I do it just because my boss/teacher/other authority figure wants me too?"

"How boring! There are a million other things I would rather be doing."

"I don't even know where to start!" or "It's just too overwhelming !"

"I'm never going to do it to my satisfaction."

"I have so many great ideas, but I'm not sure where to begin!"

"What if things go wrong?" or "What if I royally mess up?"

When you love freedom and take responsibility for your living you don't like doing anything you are obligated to do. You don't like the feeling of others having control over you.

We are in present....it means we are not lost ;) ....but because we forget to notice ourselves...we think are lost ...we are exactly who we are here and now....revisiting the past is about getting more understanding of who you were and how that link with what you want here and now ....also looking into the future is to help you get the sense of where you want to be and how you can get there.....

Most importantly is about here and now living peaceful and feeling loved while you work on the detailed plan about where you want to be......that's why freedom is so important to people who work towards being happy here and now.

Happy means when you have used your inner power to feel peaceful and loved all the times and face the outside world with the eyes of inner-love you feel. Success is to achieve that happiness I described and maintain it through life journey here and now.

Have you ever really thought about what SUCCESS means to you? Many people want to be successful, but have no other definition than their job, money or other more material things. But have you also noticed that when chasing success many people get lost in their lives.

The reason for this is that people don't have a good definition of success and do not have an integrated approach to success AND happiness.

# Exercise

## Answers

Holistic Spiritual Approach of MM will help you to define your success with 11 basic questions if you already have not defined it through the exercises we did so far:

What is most important value in life for you?

What do you love about you, life and the world?

What do you need to be happy here and now all the times.... even when you face difficult situations?

What is most important thing in life that you cannot live with out?

What do you need in order to feel in peace and love here and now?

What does the world need?

What can you be paid for?

What are you plans to create the reality you want?

# Exercise

# Answers

Holistic Spiritual Approach of
MM will help you to define
your success with 11 basic
questions if you already have
not defined it through the
exercises we did so far:

What do you need to create the
reality you want and in same
time to feel happy here and now
....not wait for tomorrow to feel
good?

How your younger self will love
about life?

Before you die .....how would
you like your movie about your
life journey to be?

Answering these questions will
let you find your mission, your
passion, your vocation and your
profession. It will help you to
find your purpose in life.

240

**Exercises** where you learn how to travel safe in your past to a painful experiences and help yourself to heal through understanding and pure love you have created here and now.

**Stage one:** is where you observe your past life journey but don't do nothing more .....is like you are on the sea where cant swim but only have the head out of the water to breath while the whole body is under the water.

**Stage two:** is where you can go on deep water just to look under the water but not swim yet. So at this stage you may chose a particular experience and spend some time with that pain or just visit whole past life journey in more depth where you take time to understand the pain or other experience in more depth.

**Stage three:** is the stage where you can swim for how long you need with out no worries, fear or feel pain as you now have learned to show full love to your whole past life journey so far and in this stage you are fully transformed spiritualy and your fear has been turned into pure love.

We all come up against roadblocks in life, big and small. Depending on our mood, or level of strength and vitality, they can feel overly complex or daunting. And can grow vast in size in our minds. And so procrastination kicks in.

Here's how to go into "pre-crastination" instead and confidently move toward a desired outcome.

This is a neat little roadmap you can use to overcome a challenge.

It is predicated on the fact that "the challenge" is a challenge as such only in your mind -- so the first part is to soften and heal and optimise your internal representation of it.

After you heal yourself from the thoughts and emotions that don't serve your peace and love here and now ....you will be able to activate your Higher Self/inner Genius to see the challenge already overcome (Vision) and to see the best way to overcome it (Strategy).

**Be present.....deep breath ....take in the smell of life: Goal, affirmation and love stages of MM will be blended at this topic**

I noticed that when you are under influence of your soul and intuition you are not using your mind or heart....which means you don't remember anything apart from what you want to ask the soul and intuition.....and the soul will be able to tell things that you need at that moment....things that really serves you ...same goes for the intuition....that's why I know that when you are guided by your soul and intuition you will forget things .....Because your mind is not in use and you are fully allowing your self to relax.....if you notice this with your full awareness and use it in your favour...you will grow spiritually....if you panic when you forget things and ignore the fact that you are connect to your soul and that's why you forgetting things ....then you are not use it in the right way your higher intelligence....

242

Always staying in the presence of your soul. This happens through the following two points as starter and then working on magical module:

🌹 1-Spending time at least 30min up to 2 hour a day with yourself. At least one day a week should be for you only. (When you are reflecting, that is your soul's voice. Analysis, with knowledge and answers to your questions are coming from the intuition – the voice of creator). But remember, creator never makes decisions for you but is like a therapist to you. You are only provided with answers to your questions. Sometimes, you are not given answers because it is not time yet, or maybe you need to learn something in the meantime. This time alone is to help you feel home.....in peace and feel loved here and now.....also notice everything you need to notice to help you enjoy the momen fully and work on your best abilities for tomorrow aims and goals.

🌹 2- Surround yourself with or meet people that that speak to you the truth through love.
These are the main food that give you more options on guide you where to get the food for love such as nature, good friends, family, children, work, home etc. They also help you to prioritise the best options.

The difference between soul-relationship, attraction-relationship, good-relationships and the right relationships need to be understand and aware as that can complicate things and unbalance your self-love.

🌹 Relationship with yourself
🌹 Relationship with others around you
🌹 Relationship with your family
🌹 Creating the right one in order to get the right one

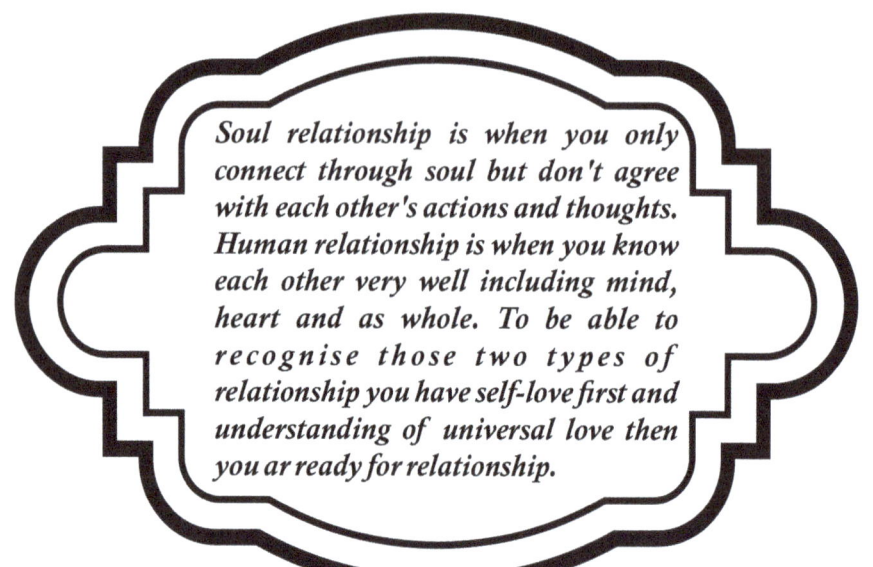

*Soul relationship is when you only connect through soul but don't agree with each other's actions and thoughts. Human relationship is when you know each other very well including mind, heart and as whole. To be able to recognise those two types of relationship you have self-love first and understanding of universal love then you ar ready for relationship.*

**How to practice the spread of love even in dark moments?** When the world turns upside down e.g. something unexpected happens such as losing a loved one, losing a home, losing a health, ending up in prison without being your fault ... etc.

How self-love can help you to understand and overcome the most difficult moments of your life? Exercise imagining the worse thing can happen to you, write down your thoughts and feelings before the exercise and after to notice the difference.

The breathing needs to be practiced, that by breathing you can go to the soul and contact with creator for guidance. 5 times deep breath, then 5 more dep breaths with awarness of your whole your inner world and outside world........can be continued until you have regulated your breath and have reached to your higher energy......centere of you.....in top of your head is your full atention and guidance.....

By trusting your soul and the creator link to your purpose. Believe everything happens for a better reason......have a deep discussion once you have conected to your higher energy....

If the self-love guidance are not applied, then you have to analyse your behaviours. You have to interact with your soul and creator to find out why it happened and what will be learned to curry in the right way, on the road to finding peace and love, because your life does not end but still exists. If you decide to end your life with your will it means you are giving up on you and your life journey and is not fulfilling the purpose of coming to this life. Long and deep discussion that lead to solution and action plan.....

Remember, remember and remember. You were born alone in this world and for a purpose. You are special, remember to believe in your light: your purpose. Remember you know why you came into this life journey. Simply go deeper into depth, going beyond your being and being one with your soul. There you will be full of strength, love, and you see that everything is happening for something better.

---

**Exercise:** Once you are connected to your soul you are able to see the challenges as adventures and use it to grow:

Look at it as a personal challenge; even if it's not something that fascinates you, what can you learn from the experience? Think of the reason why you are doing it ....why you are part of that challenge?

Post your mission statement somewhere (on your mirror, in your wallet, on your computer monitor) and read it regularly. Remind yourself why you want to accomplish the task. Create a good motivational quote.

Look at it one step at a time if the big picture is too much for you to handle. Break it down into a detailed list of each step, and get started on the small tasks.

Balance your energy and recharge your energy : Incorporate stress-relieving tactics into your work schedule. (Whatever works for you; music, hot bath, a walk, meditation, sports, writing poetry...)

✿ Keep perspective by looking back at other "jobs" you found overwhelming; in the end, they probably weren't as bad as you originally thought. After all, you lived! Make a list of what you have "survived" to remind yourself of your resilience.

✿ Organise yourself/mind, heart, body and time alone: Is there anything in your schedule that can be postponed or cancelled to open up some time? Learn to PRIORITIZE; make a list of everything you have to accomplish, then order them according to the most important. Get those done before you even dream of tackling the others.

✿ Ask for help, Learn to say "no". Sometimes you have to be a little selfish and put limits on what you can do with out hurting others.

✿ Develop shortcuts for the things you already learned ....

✿ Reminder of self-love: Reward yourself. Plan to give yourself a nice bonus when the job is completed.

✿ Include elements of fun in the task by accepting the reason why you choose to do it in the first place. Focus on your long-term objectives, the REASON why you have to do this task. Buy a day planner, plug in a schedule with sufficient "reward" breaks after periods of work.

✿ Eliminate as many distractions as you can from your surroundings. Feed with love commitment: Talk to someone you can trust about your fears – getting them out might help you put them behind you when you feel giving up...remind yourself of your strengths.

✿ Combine your passion with self-love: Set deadlines for the time you will spend on each task, so if you are obsessing over details you have to just stop and let them go.

🌸 Reflect/analyse/be realistic and love your decisions: Rather than getting all pie-eyed over an idea, take a realistic look at the steps to achieving a task. Are they really realistic? Are they worth all the effort? If they are, go for it…but be prepared for all the hard work involved! Have a back-up plan.

🌸 Be here and now….in moment: Post your Mission Statement somewhere you will see it every day to remind you WHY you want to accomplish the task in order to feel good when you work on it. Put your own personal touch on everything you decide to do, so you feel like you giving love and automatically you will receive love from universe ….it is all about sharing love and living in love …..use a certain talent or strength to your full advantage.

*By the way: As a little extra motivator, sign a contract with yourself. You can ask someone to witness the official signing…preferably someone who will remind you about it from time to time! We need to have a structure of self discipline in place in order to make sure we are following what we love doing and we don't get lost in fear.*

### VERY IMPORTANT:

Now transfer the steps of the Plan to your Day-Timer or calendar, somewhere you will see them daily. Do one thing on that list TODAY. Get the ball rolling and don't stop! Or create your own lists of motivation and love you have for challenges, strategies how to look at challenges as adventure to keep living your life journey with love.

Vision your future and be clear why you love that vision......create clear action plan how to heal yourself from the past, how to be in peace and felled love here and now and have the right tools to work on your future vision:
All the stages of MM will be blended at this topic.

## KEEPING THE BALANCE OF FIRST TWO TOPICS YOU EXPLORED EARLIER

**Exercise as homework**:

Keeping a daily diary of your thoughts and emotions

Creating a detailed plan to achieve your goals and how to follow it daily

Write reflection, evaluation of your work towards your goals daily....how did you do it and what can you do better or more

Write a letter to your self when you were happy and gad everything in control....write to Express your pain .....pay attention to any thoughts may come during this exercise and write it down....then this exercise needs a follow up work

People will hate you because they don't know better,
rate you because they love distraction
shake you because they satisfy their mind and heart,
and break you because they don't operate from love energy,
But SELF-LOVE WILL GUIDE YOU AND HELP YOU TO FEEL LOVED WHETVER SITUATION YOU ARE FACING

> "If you want to achieve your goals...keep your enemies close so you know their moves and can prepare your self for victory "

Exercise to demonstrate how self-love will protect you when working with others:

🌸 Plan / organization

🌸 Calming and staying in high energy

🌸 Listen to intuition all the time

🌸 Up and down emotionally through experiencing the pain of other

🌸 Self-control that does not alloy to interfere my heart and mind

🌸 Focussed on Purpose while walking on the darkness of reality

🌸 Facing the frequencies of others and singing the song I think may be useful ...keep your frequency

🌸 Facing achievement.... shock .....enjoy it, understand it...

🌸 The meaning of all the points above what was done and how it was done ..... a couple of hours of reflection

Then listening to someone melody that lays deep into your heart but cannot show comfort because intuition says the person need strength ......listening to your intuition guidance

Inside me the heart is crying and intuition holds the strengths is need it and speaks ...trust your intuition and your abilities to be transparent

Keep the pain of the painful melody in silence ....in silence comfort that pain, embrace it, hugs it and heal it through love energy ..... also pray for strength to work....be a healer through pure love

*Take each of the points and demonstrate how you have applied to your daily life since you started the Mentoring Programme / write your reflection / your inner discussion / your intuition guidance / your conclusion of the exercise and your inner discussion.*

To work in desires .... you must love your life and the reason you live ....

Be happy here and now .....when you decide you search for answers.....but have to be 100% practicing purity as if you don't then your answers will be blurry and wrong ones ....because Creator has created us pure and we must maintain that purity in order to be happy here and now and have clear vision of our goals ........at this point my mentor has been for free .....and has been my Creator and life on itself with anything that had thrown at me ......

One of my reflection on my self as I was struggling to work in the standard I want on my last book and come up with those points below:

To work on your wishes need to love deeply life and the reason why you want to live and I need it to work on points below.......

 over and over again

🌸 on the purposes

🌸 in reminder of motivation

🌸 in the commitment plan

🌸 in the love of desires/purpose

🌸 in love for yourself, others and life

🌸 Daily reflection

🌸 analysis of doing the right thing to yourself and others

🌸 to love yourself even when you are different or choose to be different .....

🌸 seek opinions and help from those that you value ....

🌸 spend time with the children who have been feed it from pure love by their parents ....so they can give you some and remind you of the feeling of higher energy......the love here and now....joy ...

🌸 express the suspicions and the foolishness that your mind and heart will say and don't block it but consider it and discuss it in order to heal those feelings and show them the right way or let them go in the universe if they don't' serve you....

🌸 to be sheltered in nature

🌸 ask nature for the energy you need ..... embrace and enter the world of nature

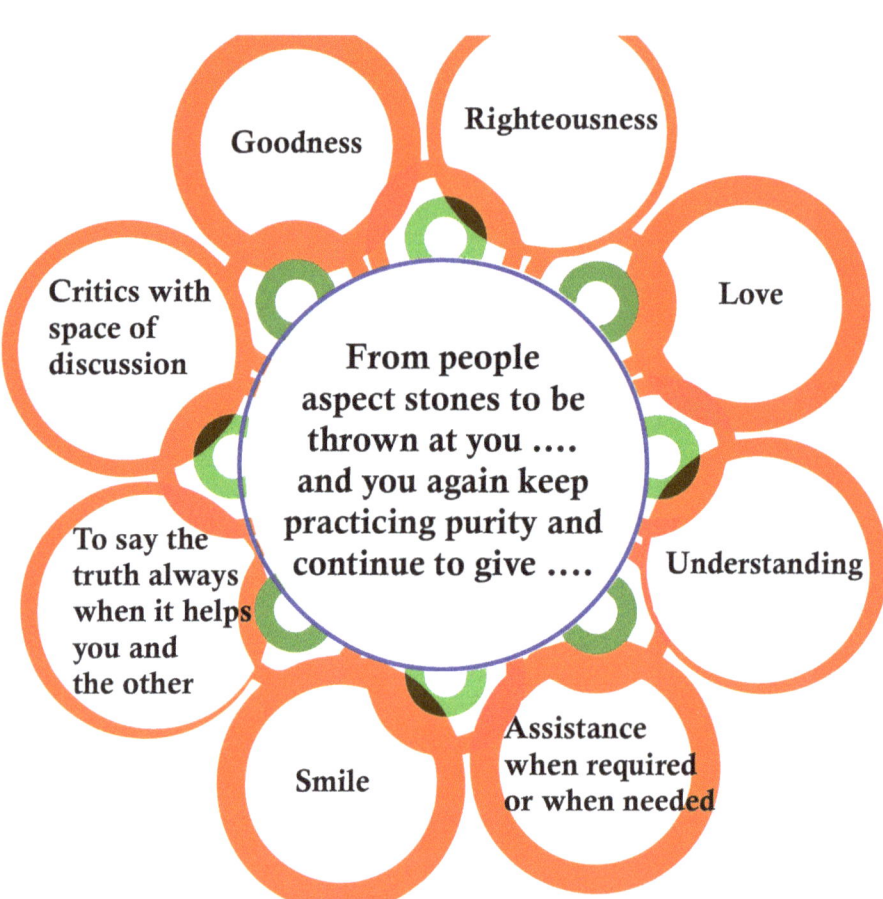

Goodness

Righteousness

Critics with space of discussion

Love

From people aspect stones to be thrown at you .... and you again keep practicing purity and continue to give ....

To say the truth always when it helps you and the other

Understanding

Smile

Assistance when required or when needed

❋ Communication with yourself and with the creator does not cost anything and is free, so there are really no excuses. If you ask for his guidance he will be there. You can only expect him to be there if you are specific about what you need, what you want and why you need it. Listening to the creator is a skill which needs to be learned and can be obtained through practice. You simply need silence and time. I previously explained this example, which is similar to my theory. There are numerous layers which need to be explored in depth, in order to learn more about the key factors- self-love and communication skills and that's why my programmes are general that has space for creativity and personalisation depending on what your bring. ❋

Self–love, the key to everything

Create the life on your own beliefs

Where the self-love exists, only love and understanding will be applied

## Loving yourself:

1- Learn to accept and love yourself for who you are and the way you are. Analyse what you do not like about yourself and plan how you're going to change or make improvements. Alternatively, you can accept these flaws and not complain about them.

An individual who wants to be loved does not waste time on overthinking, complaining, moaning, wanting what others have, not liking their image, wanting others to love them, judging others, talking about others when it does not benefit the person they are talking about, wanting more money , etc. Accepting yourself means allowing yourself to show compassion and understanding towards the person you are and having deep conversations with yourself in order to discover who you want to be. You need to go through the stages of momentum and acceptance in order to completely understand this point and ultimately achieve it.

**Exercise:** Write down …..your thoughts about statement, your inner work evaluation so far, what else you need to improve, what is stopping you to be 100% happy here and now, what are your complains and negative thoughts…..

2- What we give energy to, that is what we attract. If you focus your energy on all your problems then those problems will follow you. Alternatively, if you focus your energy on finding solutions then these solutions will become a part of you. When seeking solutions, quietly step back in order to view the whole the situation, the problem or the issue that is presented as a whole picture. We have to show compassion and consideration to the whole of us before we decide on a solution. Refer to the goal stage for more details at MM PROGRAM.

**Exercise: Write down .....your thoughts about statement, your inner work evaluation so far, what else you need to improve, what is stopping you to be 100% happy here and now, what are your complains and negative thoughts.....RATE YOUR ENERGY 1 TO 10 AND EXPLAIN THE GAB IF IT IS A GAB.**

3- Let go of the things that hold you back from being yourself. Once you start to be a product of justice towards yourself and others, it is difficult for you to stay around those who don't practice the same justice towards themselves and others. This is because you want to be truthful and being truthful requires lots of energy and skills, in order to learn when and how to be honest without hurting others. Until you learn how to be truthful and you practice justice you must keep your distance from those who complicate your journey or become obstacles.

Exercise: Write down .....your thoughts about statement, your inner work evaluation so far, what else you need to improve, what is stopping you to be 100% happy here and now, what are your complains and negative thoughts.....

4- Be aware of all the negative obstacles but focus on the goal. Be aware of the fear that you are feeling. Talk to the fear so that you can understand it and reassure it that you have a plan. It is through your inner conversations that you can make the following points happen:

— Turn pain into compassion and understanding.

— Turn fear into a plan, as you become more aware of what your fear is telling you.

— Turn anxiety into self belief.

— Turn loneliness into the comfort of your pure love and dance through your pure love.

— Allow your soul to be a healer of your mind and heart through your inner discussions.

**Exercise: Write down .....your thoughts about statement, your inner work evaluation so far, what else you need to improve, what is stopping you to be 100% happy here and now, GIVE ONE EXAMPLE FOR EACH POINT HOW YOU CAN SHIFTED INTO GOOD ENERY.....**

5- Ensure that you are clear about your visions in life and frequently revisit them. Make sure that you live 100% in the present, so that you can fully enjoy everything you do in the moment. This involves being 80% productive at what you do in the present and 5% revisiting the past if you require any lessens or any good memories. Furthermore, the remaining 15% is dedicated to future visions and to moving forward to get to where you want to be.

**Exercise: Write down .....your thoughts about statement, your inner work evaluation so far, what else you need to improve, what is stopping you to be 100% happy here and now, CREATE YOUR FUTURE VISION MAP.....**

6- Dream big, visualise your dreams, and break them in small goals. Loving yourself is the most amazing thing that I have discovered and it is something which has helped my clients be content, appreciate what they have, learn to feel loved within, know with who to share universal love, know which kind of partner they want , how to treat others through compassion and understanding, planning for their goals, making time for themselves, noticing the little things that make them happy, valuing themselves, believing in their abilities, understanding what others say and do, and smiling to themselves in the mirror and to the world.

**Exercise: NOW ADD TO THE MAP EACH STEP THAT WILL TAK YOU THERE AND THE RESOURCES YOU NEED.......**

7- Your intuition and your soul provide you with guidance. Ensure that you find time to listen and have conversations daily. Don't just start a conversation and then simply ignore it because it is deep and needs more energy, attention, focus, will, determination, creativity on questions asked, curiosity of seeing things in all areas that can benefit you and your life journey, including others involved, ensure you reach the end of the conversation with you eventually come to a conclusion, plan and out it into action.

Exercise: LETS HAVE THAT INNER CONVERSATION ABOUT YOUR FUTURE VISION MAP AND COME UP WITH MORE INPUT INCLUDING TIME SCALE FOR EACH STEP WHEN TO START AND WHEN TO FINISH IT......

8- Pursue your passion and find a job you love and enjoy so that you give your best. Through those inner conversations, you have to discover the ways you can pursue your passion and enjoy the job you have decided to do. Remember we have one life which we need to enjoy and make the most. Have those inner conversations daily and as often as you need. End these conversations with reflections, analysis and actions?

Exercise: Write down.... YOUR LOVE FOR EACH STEP AND FOR WHOLE FUTURE VISION MAP WHAT IT MEANS TO YOU HERE AND NOW........ALSO ADD A BACK UP PLAN FOR FLEXIBILITY THAT INCLUDES MINIMUM THREE OPTIONS

9- Consistently surround yourself with things that are meaningful to you.

— Know who to socialise with, as you are meant to share universal love. Those who have not discovered self-love are unable to share love, instead they will just feed on your self love. You should be aware of this and make decisions accordingly.

— Ensure you have a purpose regardless of how you choose to spend your time. Your time is the key to your peace, love and creating the reality you want and enjoying the moment.

— Have daily inner conversations in order to evaluate how your day went and reflect on what you did, what you wanted to do or what you could have done.

Exercise: ADD TO THE MAP THE PEOPLE YOU LIKE TO INCLUDE IN YOUR LIFE JOURNEY AND GIVE REASONS WHY.....

🌼 10- Ensure that you live your life only for yourself and no one else; it is yours and only you can decide how to live it. Every time you feel like something is not going the way you want, you have to stop all the thoughts, all the emotions and just connect with your higher power, with your soul, your creator and see everything from their point of view. You will understand why you are important and why it is important to make yourself satisfied from a pure love point of view and not an ego point of view. Your achievement of pure love cannot benefit other, unless you help them achieve it from within. We are here to help ourselves, not to rely on others. Of course others can help us move forward and climb our steps a bit faster, but that's it. So help which does not help the individual to help themselves in not beneficial, except for when you know that your help is helping them to progress two or three steps forward. This is why it is important to focus on being content, without relying on others. It is only when you are content that you can help others in the correct way.

Exercise: Write down .....your thoughts about statement, your inner work evaluation so far, what else you need to improve, what is stopping you to be 100% happy here and now, what are your complains and negative thoughts.....THINK OF THE OPTION ACHIVING IT ALONE THAT LIFE JOURNEY MAP......WRITE DOWN THE PLAN AND HOW WILL HELP YOU TO BE HAPPY HERE AND NOW ?

🌼 11- Believe in your uniqueness and the universe will guide you. Remember if you can't accept and love yourself just the way you are you will not have confidence, high self esteem, lots of doubts and not sure that you deserve what your vision is. Easy could be alloying yourself to feel for those who keep buttering you. So you need to have a serious conversation with your soul to find ways how to feel loved and to remind yourself all the good things you have and those that you are in progress to get. Continue to reflect on your progress of the changes that you have decided to make. It's important to find ways how to feel loved through your pure love in order to shine and enjoy everything you do and you will recognize the truth from the lie, the compliment from someone who is trying to make you like them. Use of manipulation for their interest only, you will know someone who has problem with themselves but instead they put you down, you will appreciate the critics, the truth, genuinely and straightforward people.

Exercise: CREATE THREE TO FIVE QUOTES THAT WILL REMIND YOU YOUR INNER STREGTH IN THE MOMENTS WHEN YOU FEEL GIVING UP, EVALUATING THINGS and difficult challenges you may face.....

12- Treat everyone the way you like to be treated, to receive the same from the universe. This is very important and need lots of awareness, attention, and reflection from the soul and creator point of view. Also needs healing time for your mind and heart after each situation that did not feel right to you. Healing can be done through your soul by allowing your soul to be the therapist for your thoughts and feelings. Moreover reflect daily through your inner conversations on how you have dealt with others from whole you but the soul and creator has to have the last say if you trust your soul and the creator. Sometimes we follow their guidance even without being clear or making sense but later we will understand.

Exercise: CREATE THREE TO FIVE QUOTES THAT WILL REMIND YOU TO TREAT OTHERS RIGHT AND GIVE THREE EXAMPLES THAT YOU MAY THINK YOU HAVE NOT TREATED OTHERS RIGHT AND WHAT YOU WILL DO DIFFERENTLY...

When you start the journey through the self-love can cure all emotional and physical illness, as you will become product of pure love. You will only be part of pure love, no judgment, no anger, no getting upset more then what is need it for healing time, don't hate anyone or anything, you will allow understand of others and show compassion. You will feel loved, never feel lonely, you will know your value and you will not accept less then what you deserve. You feel confident, strong, you will have the highest intelligence as you get information directly from the soul which knows everything and creator. You will not relay anymore on your mind and heart because your awareness has improved on observing your thoughts and feelings though the healing sessions from your soul. You can see through others and understand their actions instead of judging or getting angry as you know the ways how to get what you want in the way that is recognized by universe and others as is the language of love.

**Exercise on the ingredients of knowing if you are doing your best: Write on the list of 7 steps that you using for each points of doing your best ingredients explaining how you use it in your life…what is the outcome…what can you do different…why…**

"*Holistic Spiritual Approach on Magical Module*"

VJOLLCA SADIKU
Co- Founder & Director
Magical Coaching

# 4 Focus therapy on one problem presented

## The forty eight ingredients of knowing if you are doing your best are:
### Time scale is three months

# Focus therapy on one problem presented

## The forty eight ingredients of knowing if you are doing your best are:
### Time scale is three months

1) Awareness ......who you are, your present environment, obstacles, fears, others, happenes, meaning of your life....why you ar living for? ....write one page for each topic

2) Determination.....how much do you want, what you aiming to achive and why? Make a list

3) Using your time wisely. ...organise your time , family, friends, work, passion, passionate love, socialasing, alone time, recharging your energy.......make a plan for daily, weekly, monthly ....and long term plan ....you can add or take awy anything from the list that is not link to your life........

4) Creativity.... lets write in circle what have you created so far and what creativity gives you ?

5) Curiosity.... Write all the things that you are curiosity and the reason why.....also write down a list of what would help you to know more in order to achive your goal?.....

6) Honesty...how honest you are towards yourself, others and life? Make a list when you have not been honest and when you have been honest that has made huge influence on your life journey and in you're emotional wellbeing.........

7) Be truthful to your self and others through compassion and understanding...give me example when you have been truthful and when you have not been truthful link to your inner conversation link to your goal or problem......

8) Manage your money......make a list of your income, outcome and then organize how to spend less then what you earn, explore how much would you lik to earn and how you going to make it happen .....what are you doing to use money for what you need and to appreciate what you have ?

9) Daily inner conversation...morning conversation, during the day in auto pilot, in your breaks, your time alone, in the evenings, before you go to sleep.

10)Daily reflection of everything you did and making notes ......here you are creator of your life through love you have to use language of love in order to create the right energy and feel loved...consider wisely everything you do and with who you interact .......by asking yourself if you have done the right thing by yourself and by others.......

11) Plan....you have to look at your daily plan, weekly plan, monthly plan and long term plan to see how you getting on ......

12) Have a vision.....without a vision you will feel stuck .....tired, and depressed .....vision gives you love when you are working in that vision ......what is your vision for long term plans, monthly plans, weekly plans and daily plans......before you go to sleep your vision should be clear in order to feel loved and in peace.....

13) Get inspired.......who does inspire you? What does inspire you? How can you inspire yourself daily? How can you be inspiring for someone?

14) Indulge in your imagination of your vision.......even though you are clear in your vision ....still let your imagination play with your vision just in case you are missing any opportunity

15) Be your own critic ......learn how to be your own critic with love and understanding leaving space to have inner discussion in order to come up with best solution to change for better....

16)    Show compassion to your self......love yourself no matter what ......but be willing to change for better and the things you don't like about yourself....change is growth....is love....

17) Cry if you need to cry but find a solution and move on…everything has a solution and reason for happening…..understand what is happening, learn, grow, allow yourself to explore your emotions and thoughts and look beyond what is represented …..

18) Reflect on your plans……be focused, disciplined, organized, flexible, and love what you do ….

19) Reflect on your actions……write down the things that are not clear and don't make sense to you, share it with a right friend, write down your free thoughts and feelings bout it, have inner conversation when you are thinking about those experiences but don't overthinking if you com to a conclusion or if you don't have something new to add to that inner conversation ……your mind and your energy is importance…..don't use it for the things that don't bring peace and love

20) Reflect/evaluate your thoughts and feelings……..is everything you doing maintaining your peace and love? Are you hurting anyone else with your actions? "if you getting hurt is because you still need to do inner work…..and is only you to be blamed for the pain you feeling" ….

21) Be best friends with the creator….he is there all the times to guide you when you need guidance, when you feel unloading, when you need clarification, when you just need someone to love you, you can discuss with him anything you feel to discuss and

anything that is bothering you …..he is there for you to help you be happy here and now and help you achieve the reality you want……prayers don't help if you don't have deep discussion with him….including the reason of the prayer and what you are hoping to achieve with that prayer and why….

22) Put yourself first…..if you are not happy here and now all the times …it mean's you are not putting yourself first and you are not helping anyone……so what is the point of your actions? Explain to yourself what is happening….

23) Focus on your goal and purpose……what are you doing to achieve your goal? What can you do more? Create at least three affirmation why you love that goal and purpose of the goal? ……put the time scale on achieving each step of the goal…consider the resources you need and how you going to get them ….create details plans …

24) Demand that you are a product of justice towards yourself and ask the creator how to get what you need…….show the universe that you are doing the right thing by yourself and others in order to get what you aiming for ….or asking why you are not getting what you are aiming to get ……because w meant to get what we deserve ……100% we meant to be happy here and now all the times …..and work hard to create the reality we want.

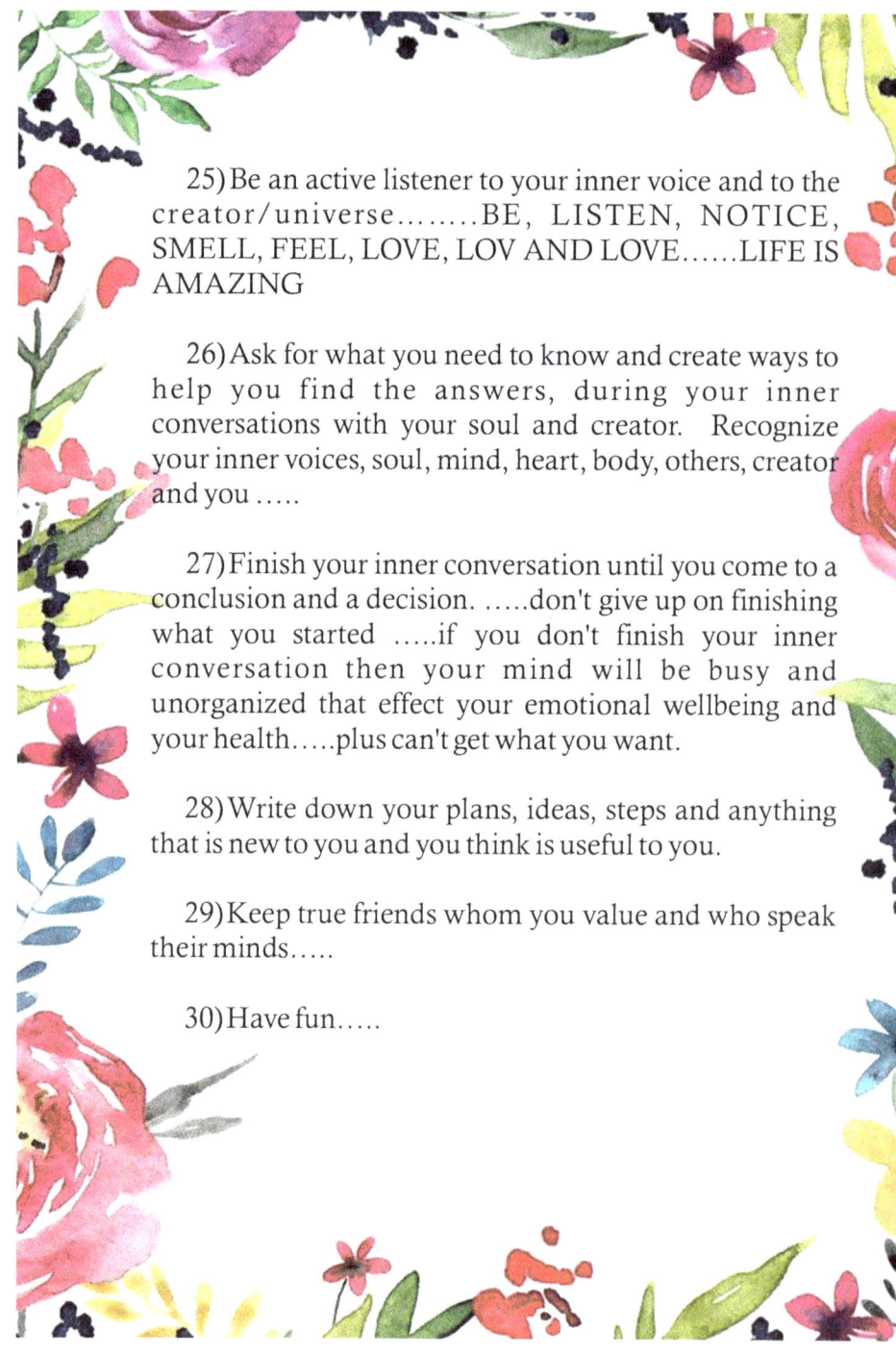

25) Be an active listener to your inner voice and to the creator/universe........BE, LISTEN, NOTICE, SMELL, FEEL, LOVE, LOV AND LOVE......LIFE IS AMAZING

26) Ask for what you need to know and create ways to help you find the answers, during your inner conversations with your soul and creator. Recognize your inner voices, soul, mind, heart, body, others, creator and you .....

27) Finish your inner conversation until you come to a conclusion and a decision. .....don't give up on finishing what you started .....if you don't finish your inner conversation then your mind will be busy and unorganized that effect your emotional wellbeing and your health.....plus can't get what you want.

28) Write down your plans, ideas, steps and anything that is new to you and you think is useful to you.

29) Keep true friends whom you value and who speak their minds.....

30) Have fun.....

31) Look after you body, mind and heart through your soul guidance.....eat healthy, exercise, stay in higher energy, clean your energy every time you come from outside world into your inner world, look after your emotions...heal them and turn into love any hurtful emotions.... listen to your thoughts from your mind and take care of them......

32) Ask for help when you think you need it.......even if you don't get help ....you still ask for help if it feels right to ask.....but allays only rely on your self....

33) Never rely on others........create strategies how to have lots of affirmations and enough resources to be able to look after yourself .....remember we only need ourselves to have anything we need .......be happy, practice purity, asked to be loved within, be a good friend with creator and work hard for what you aim for ....that's all....

34) Trust but be aware of not trusting and as soon as you see signs of doubt, keep it in back of your mind until you can prove it.

35) Only trust your soul and creator.

36) Believe that everything happens for a reason, thus you have to discover it or just keep going if it feels right.

37) Accept the unknown and develop the right skills to learn how to deal with it. The unknown is a part of our journey and the beauty of life.

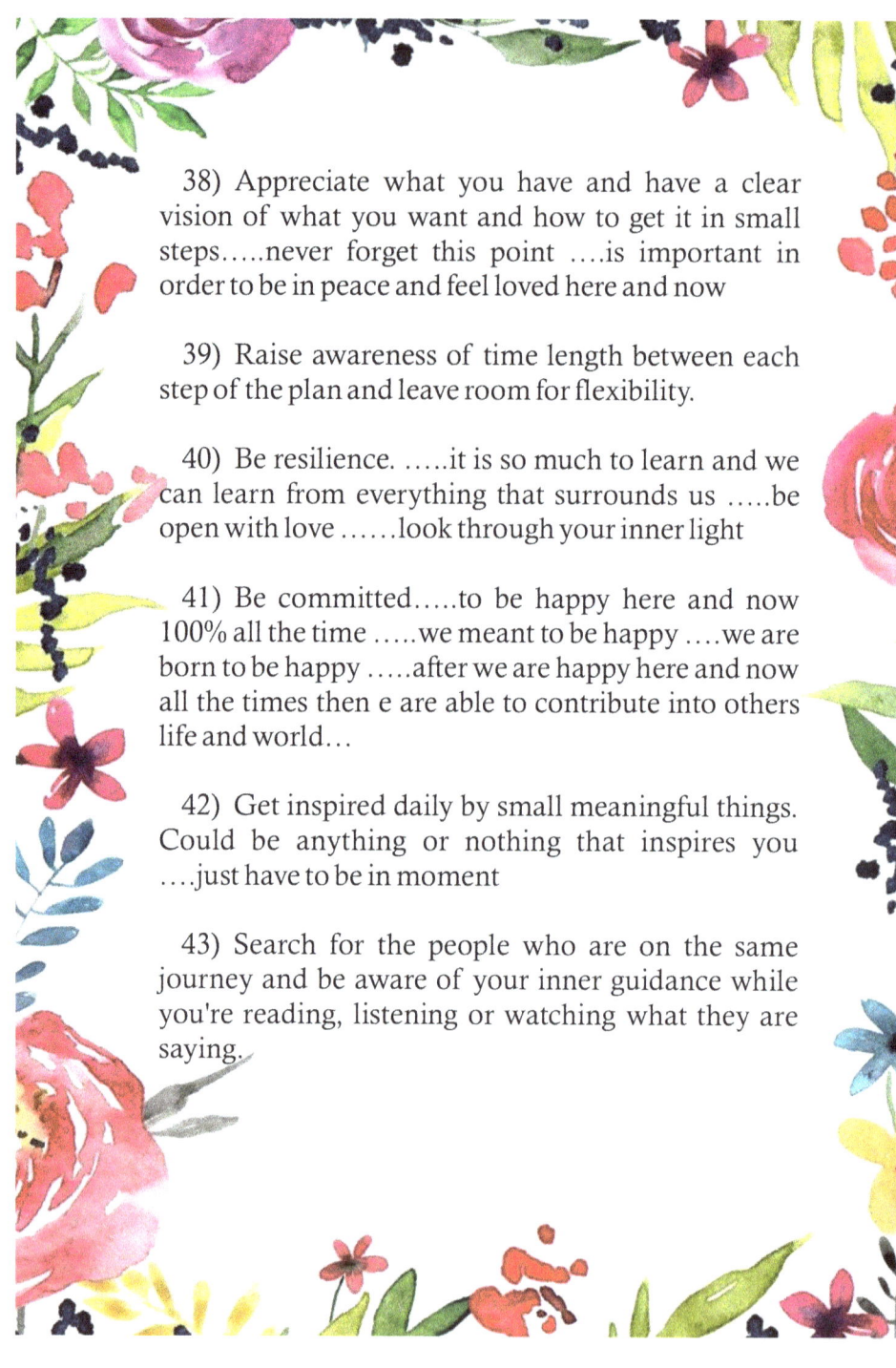

38) Appreciate what you have and have a clear vision of what you want and how to get it in small steps…..never forget this point ….is important in order to be in peace and feel loved here and now

39) Raise awareness of time length between each step of the plan and leave room for flexibility.

40) Be resilience. …..it is so much to learn and we can learn from everything that surrounds us …..be open with love ……look through your inner light

41) Be committed…..to be happy here and now 100% all the time …..we meant to be happy ….we are born to be happy …..after we are happy here and now all the times then e are able to contribute into others life and world…

42) Get inspired daily by small meaningful things. Could be anything or nothing that inspires you ….just have to be in moment

43) Search for the people who are on the same journey and be aware of your inner guidance while you're reading, listening or watching what they are saying.

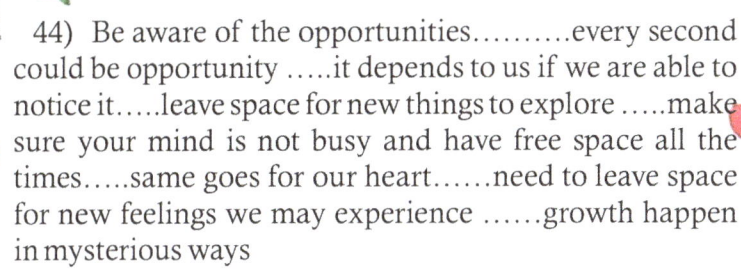

44) Be aware of the opportunities..........every second could be opportunity .....it depends to us if we are able to notice it.....leave space for new things to explore .....make sure your mind is not busy and have free space all the times.....same goes for our heart......need to leave space for new feelings we may experience ......growth happen in mysterious ways

45) Say sorry when you know that you are in the wrong........ say sorry , think ways how to put it right, and don't worry just keep moving forward.....

46) Desire...... desire in order....1-happenes within, 2- to feel loved within, 3- to do the right thing by others, 4- to dream big and go for it .....fly....

47) Will...... dream, visualize, believe, plan and get into action ......love what you do

48) Analysis of the options you have......life does not end when you achieve to be happy 100% here and now ....but it upgrades to different level if you like to consider different options of growth......

"Holistic Spiritual Approach on Magical Module"

VJOLLCA SADIKU
Co- Founder & Director
Magical Coaching

# 5 Youth Program 16 to 18... or 25 years old...

# Youth Program 16 to 18... or 25 years old...

This programme is introduction to MM coaching programme or Mentoring programme and time scale is one month. The reason I left it free to flow by young person is because ......I feel their confusion, fear, desperation to feel loved, scared of the future, hurt when they think of the people they love.....etc....etc .....and I know they will feel it each step of MM with their passion, imagination, essence of love, and lots of different dreams including amazing courage and inspiration. They are our future and we have to support them to be in the path they dream of being.

**Momentum stage:** Tell me what is happening ....

**Exercise:** Write down 11 things that are going wrong, how would you like to be going and what can be done in your side to make the change, also who else is involved on the changes that you think need to happen in order to have things how you want?

**Exercise:** Write 11 things that are going well in your life and how you can keep maintaining them to go well....

**Acceptence:** Let's see the options are available and what we have to thank you for.....

Write 21 things that you are thankfully for ....and why....

**Goal:** Exploring the goals you like to achieve, your future vision, the fun here and now, and your list of the things you like to achieve here and now, tomorrow, in a week time, in one month time and in long term .....

**Write 5 main goals**
**10 sub goals**

Categorise them in time scale and why you love them to achieve......explain each step towards achieving the goal

**Inspiration:** What does inspire you and how you have been getting inspiration up to now? How important is for you to be inspiration for others and also to be inspired by yourself, others and life?

Write things that inspire you about yourself, who else inspire you and why.....

**Commitment:** How committed you are to be "you", to do the right thing by yourself and others? To be happy here and now all the times 100%? To feel in peace and feeling loved all the times? To create the reality you really want? To find out what you really want?

**Write 5 strategies** that have been working so far to help you be committed to something you wanted.....and **create 5 more strategies** to help you be committed to what you have found it challenging to commit.

**Affirmation:** Create a list of affirmations for you that it resonates with you, with your strength, with what you have achieved so far, (write 5 or 10 for each topic) with all the good qualities you own, with all the vision you have, based on your values, and who you want to be.....for each affirmation create a action plan with details of what you like to achieve and the time scale when to start and when to finish it ......reasons why you love your plans and three other possibilities if anything goes wrong with the plans ......

**Love:** Tell me how you define love, how much love you have got so far, how much love you have given away...would you like to know how to be loved all the times by yourself? And have lots of love to give away?

"*Holistic Spiritual Approach on Magical Module*"

VJOLLCA SADIKU
Co- Founder & Director
Magical Coaching

# 6 Fostering HSAOMM Program / Foster Carer and Child

….time scale for this programme may take between one year and three years to achieve the outcomes of HSAOMMP.

# Fostering HSAOMM Program /
# Foster Carer and Child

## ....time scale for this programme may take between one year and three years to achieve the outcomes of HSAOMMP.

This programme is just summery of structure of the programme as it has to be designed and personalised based on individual cases.....as each case is unique. For more details you can look the depth content of holistic spiritual approach of magical module programme to have understanding of the purpose the programme have.

**Momentum stage:** Time scale is one month for this stage.... Tell me what is happening ....we write down everything what we want and aspect from each other.....create an agreement that suits both everyone involved.....be clear about areas that need improving and working on in order to be here and now.....

The holistic spiritual approach of MM assessment is need it in order to have e detailed and clear plan how to support the foster career and the wellbeing of the child......

Once that is done then we can move to next stage of MM.

The assessment will be created around wellbeing of the child and what support is out there to speed up to fulfil the child's needs in order for the child to enjoy life here and now and progress towards their potential.

**Acceptance:** Time scale is three months blended with other stages together in order to be ready to start working on the goal stage and achieving self-love.

Let's see the options are available and what we have to thank you for.....

Need to take into consideration: appreciation of everything we have, have deep understanding of our existence, actions of others and how life works.

Need to be a clear plan based on the assessment done on momentum stage in order to design a personalised support plan around wellbeing of the child.

Here will be introduction of self-love and start of work towards gaining self-love for both parties but mainly for the child......

The focus on foster carer will be to build healthy relationship with the child and to keep progress of the child moving....

**Goal:** Time scale for goal, inspiration and commitment stage blended with parts of affirmation and love stage will be six months intense work as will be working on the child's past thoughts and emotions in order to bring the child to enjoy here and now and keep progressing with small steps towards their potential.

With child: Exploring the goals you like to achieve, your future vision, the fun here and now, and your list of the things you like to achieve here and now, tomorrow, in a week time, in one month time and in long term …..

With foster carer: will be working on the areas the foster carer needs support and how to keep the healthy relationship with child going…..

**Inspiration:** What does inspire you and how you have been getting inspiration up to now? How important is for you to be inspiration for others and also to be inspired by yourself, others and life?

This stage will be important to be explored by both, foster carer and the child as it does support the wellbeing of the child in so many directions.

This stage is to give the child the boost it need it in order to believe in their potential and wanting the best for themselves.

**Commitment:** How committed you are to be "you", to do the right thing by yourself and others? To be happy here and now all the times 100%? To feel in peace and feeling loved all the times? To create the reality you really want ?
To find out what you really want?

**Affirmation:** Time scale for affirmation and love stage is one to two months.

Create a list of affirmations for you that it resonates with you, with your strength, with what you have achieved so far, with all the good qualities you own, with all the vision you have, based on your values, and who you want to be.....for each affirmation create a action plan with details of what you like to achieve and the time scale when to start and when to finish it ......reasons why you love your plans and three other possibilities if anything goes wrong with the plans ......

This stage will be powerful to work in both ....foster carer and the child.

**Love:** Tell me how you define love, how much love you have got so far, how much love you have given away...would you like to know how to be loved all the times by yourself? And have lots of love to give away?
At this stage I would prefer to work on self-love ingredients if the foster carer and the child agrees...because it is very important to have deep understanding of practising self-love daily .......in order to keep the balance of the harmony, peace and love here and now.

## Important of having and practising daily self-love before you become a parent.....

To be a parent with out you being self educated (not having knowledge of self-love) is like you just growing with the child.....and that may be dangers as you are not reflecting on your work as a parent but just getting on with it as life keeps you moving ...........this can have so many different turns ....that may lead to a child not achieving fully the self-love which will affect their adulthood........and to help the child get back in truck needs lots of work as their are few factors involved in the progress (parents karma, child's karma and the present energy.....)

## But if the parent has gained the self-love then the parenthood should be similar to the stages below:

✻ **Stage one:** getting ready to be a parent is the most amazing time of your life.........

✻ **Stage two:** 9 months pregnancy is the magical journey that is full of passion and love.....(I remember being in high energy all the time.....it was just amazing)

✻ **Stage three:** giving birth .....challenge that makes you think how much you really want to be a parent....is a reminder of challenges you will have to go through as a parent.....is a test....to be ready ....

✻ **Stage four:** just magical....is like you have reborn....an angel is with you ....actually is with you ....and you have an angel to guide you , To love you , To understand you, to teach you about real life and all you have to do as parent give back to that baby what they are giving you.......that's all.....they will tell you exactly how to treat them if you have self-love...you know how to understand the babies language

✻ **Stage five:** toddler......1 to 3 years old ...or even 5 years old ...depends on child growth....and development.....this age is all about being a good role model.....

✻ **Stage six:** 5 years old to 10 years old .....is the stage where the child writes their adulthood journey......which is very important stage for the child ......and if parent has self-love they will provide for the child the space to stretch their imagination through pure love

....through their soul and intuition.....in order to write the journey they come to do in this life .........(If you are adult and did not had this chance then need to have some healing in order to revisit this age....and connect with your true self)

✳ **Stage seven:** age 10th to 13th or 16th .......year old ......is the stage of teaching the child boundaries.....consequences.....true love ....in this stage take place learning of independence and growth of to understanding outside world with adult eyes.......this stage prepares the child for good start of adulthood and being confident of being adult........while they feel secure and deeply in love with themselves, life and others ......they learn .....is stage of learning and growing into adulthood

✳ **Stage eight:** 16 years old to 25 years old ......it helps them to fly into adulthood.......with out fear ....getting their dreams ....and creating the life they want .......and parent with self-love are able to pass this stage but if not they are aware of child's past life karma and still they know how to support the child to grow .........

✳ **Stage nine:** is the stage where parents have a break and enjoy their achievement as their child gets married with their true love .....happy ever after and have grand kids ..........

So this way the world will be in peace and love.......by individuals having self-love.....

Guidance from the book "Life is Magical...You are Magical"

You need to take responsibility and do the inner work to heal yourself. If you don't love yourself you will not feel loved by anyone.

Nasty behaviour is a result of unhealed pain, self-doubt, self-hatred, and self-denial. It reflects in the outer world. Commit to doing the inner work as the number 1 most important thing in your life.

Writing down all your trouble, pain, fears, negative experiences in your life every evening before bed, letting those emotions come up, cry if you can and they will be released. Do this every single night if you need too.

Youth Impact Coaching Diploma in
'There is something you must always remember.
You are braver than you believe, stronger
than you seem and smarter than you think.'

A.A. Milne

"Holistic Spiritual Approach on Magical Module"

VJOLLCA SADIKU
Co- Founder & Director
Magical Coaching

# 7 Local Authority/all Professionals.....
Holistic Spiritual Approach of Magical
Module Program.."Self-love"

Time scale can be between one months
to three months or just full one day
training just for introduction...
but for training to work need one year
to three year time scale depending
on the progress and level of requirement.

## Local Authority/all Professionals..... Holistic Spiritual Approach of Magical Module Program.."Self-love"

# Time scale can be between one months to three months or just full one day training just for introduction... but for training to work need one year to three year time scale depending on the progress and level of requirement.

Local Authorities and all professionals should be familiar with self-love ingredients of Magical Module because if they have not achieved to gain self-love then definitely their role will be not done properly and delivered with the language of love. Which mean very few people will be happy fully all the times here and now and the world will continue to be not in peace and love.

This programme will be mainly to introduce to all professionals how important is self-love, what it is self-love and how can it be achieved..... therefore will be just on paragraph for few different professions to explain why they role will make huge difference to contributing to creating and building world of peace and love if they work to gain self-love in order to be happy all the times here and now .....so then they will be able to apply pure love practice into their role of work and so on ......Become the change the world need in order to be a place of love and harmony of joy.

Some of the benefits that you get from this program are below:

Learn how to stay in the present, which can help you see things far more clearly.

Learn how to create a clear plan for the goals you wish to achieve or your work tasks.

Learn how to connect with your inner self; your true self, purify self…

Learn how to Connect With Your Highest Power…. sharpening your intuition.

Learn how to overcome the obstacles and to empower from them and how to keep applying purity love.

Learn how to understand your role at work and in life.

Learn how to love yourself in order to love others in the right way, enabling everyone to be happy.

Learn how to increase self-confidence, self believe and believe on the power of purity.

Learn how to have more courage to approach things that you still do not trust, but that you want to trust.

Learn how to Stay Realistic about your Desires and Reflect on what you really want.

Learn how to build cheerful and useful relationships, with yourself and others.

Learn how to heal yourself from your past…from the things that still are blurry.

Learn the Power of pure love and how can serve you in work and your personal life….be able to go back to your childhood and visit your future vision through imagination.

## Stage1:

Self-love ingredients to be explored through exercises in order to help you to get familiar how important is for you first to be fulfilled, in pace and feel loved with your life then know the importance of your work role.

### Intruduction to leterature reviwe on pure self-love:

According to Bandura (1986), the functioning of a human being comprises a set of reciprocal interactions between environmental, behavioural, and personal variables. The fundamental personal variable is the 'self-efficacy', or the perceived ability for acquiring or performing particular tasks at specific levels. Self-efficacy can increase successful achievements because of the individual's efforts, persistence, and as a consequence the improved performance. When compared with people, who doubt their capabilities, self-efficacious students are more likely to participate in new or challenging tasks, and appear more motivated to overcome difficulties to reach higher

285

levels (Schunk, 1999). The sense of self-efficacy is directly influenced by self-love. As individuals work on tasks where they practice and convey love, they raise their self-esteem, self-confidence and progress quicker. According to Hardy (2012) "Self-love is a state of appreciation for oneself that grows from actions that support our physical, psychological and spiritual growth. Self-love is dynamic; it grows by actions that mature us. When we act in ways that expand self-love in us, we begin to accept much better our weaknesses as well as our strengths, have less need to explain away our short-comings, have compassion for ourselves as human beings struggling to find personal meaning, are more centred in our life purpose and values, and expect living fulfilment through our own efforts". Taking responsibility for our life, choices and actions means that we have also the right to attend our needs. In this way, we can learn to love others. Being self-loving means that the person full accepts who they are, preserving their good qualities and taking continuous steps to improve the traits that they are not satisfied with. This means that the self-reproach and the resulting anxiety or distress is avoided. Instead of worrying about imperfections, the individual embraces them by also appreciating the unique strong points (Hardy, 2012). According to Cohen (2012) a happy and self-assured person, is in fact a self-lover and perceives 'the self' as a best friend, who does not demean or degrade but inspire and encourage, regardless the approval or disapproval of others (Cohen, 2012).

"If you truly loved yourself, you could never hurt another." BUDDHA

"Peace comes from within.
Do not seek it without.' Buddha

"No one saves us but ourselves. No one can and no one may. We ourselves must walk the path." Buddha

"You, yourself, as much as anybody in the entire universe, deserve your love and affection." Buddha

Further Reading/Research

David Hawkins – Map of Consciousness

Recovery of Your Inner Child by Lucia Capacchione

The 11th Element: The Key to Unlocking Your Master Blueprint for Wealth and Success by Robert Scheinfeld and Robert G. Allen (14 Oct 2003)

TA Today
Mindfulness - a practical guide to finding peace in a frantic world, Mark Williams and Danny Penman

Hay House release from Dr. Fabrizio Mancini, The Power of Self Healing

www.holisticmagicalapproach.com

Chapter two of the book "Life is Magical…You are Magical", 2018

Discuss/exercise:

-Chapter TWO on the book "Life is Magical…You are Magical" and my experience at age of 7.

-Need to ask …… what are
you thinking and where your
thinking is taking you ….

-Create an exercise to help to help you go in deep thinking …..to connect with your soul….with your pure side ….in order to come up with answers of questions below.

Let's see if we can answer those questions below including the conclusion of literature review:

**Exercise based on the information we just read to see what we all think and how can we answer the questions below…..to get deep sense of meaning of life before we start working on self –love…..**

Tell me how you describe your self?

How others will describe you?

How would you like to be described if you had a magic wound?

Can you tell me those three characters you described how can be one? If cant be one why? How can we make it to be one? Or do we need too? Or what should you do with that person that has answered those questions?

Why we are born?

Why we die?

Who control the world?

Who has created the world ?

288

What is the reason for creating the world and what is our role on it ?

How can we create a better world ?!!!!

Questions 1:

1- Are there three main rules according to the Lord?:

Treat others as you would like to be treated.

Love yourself as you would like to be loved.

Give 100% in everything that you choose.

2- Are those 3 rules, all that is required of humans to accomplish in this life? How do you explain the way that these can be applied by a person, born in a family amongst members, who do not comply with those rules?

3- For someone to follow the path that makes them happy, do they firstly have to let go of those who are not happy with themselves, or are becoming obstacles for your journey and will not allow you to achieve your dreams? Even if this encompasses their own family? What is the reason for this?

4- What is the soul? Where is it located anatomically in humans and what is the role of the soul in this life? Why...

5- Can a person live and be guided by their soul? How can this be achieved?

6 -Does a bad soul exist? The reason why…

7- Are the mind, heart and body human utensils, which serve the soul so that the person is faithful or fulfilled? Why..

8- What does it mean to believe in God and how can this be demonstrated by 3 rules or examples?

9- Do you suppose that children are like angels and innocent? Why? How is their suffering explained in God's language and why?

10- Are there two kinds of death: A prewritten one and another that depends on our Actions? If so, how is the child's death explained?

11 - Can a human-being be filled with love, which comes exclusively from the source within themselves? And from the moment they become aware of that love, they do not feel suffering because they are know their purpose and are fulfilled?

What do you think is the love within? And why do you think that way?

And discuss the answers
of others including
their answer

290

# Stage 2:

*How to learn self-love?*

*-What is love?*

Unconditional love: the meaning has to do with 3 main life rules and that they are self-love guidance.

Every love that comes from the mind and heart is false. The love that comes from the soul is true. The distinction is made if the rules below are followed and if you feel complete and in love where you are, without the need for someone else to complete you. This means you are one with your soul. If you feel lonely unhappy with these negative emotions and automatically search for someone to complete them, it means you are not connected to your soul. All of this shows and reiterates that if you love yourself, you achieve what you want and if you find that person s/he is just like yourself but you enjoy the journey together. So you have to work with yourself in order to have a healthy life, loving relationship with yourself, others and life.

## Exercise:

**Explain one example at work or your personal life where you had inner conflict because of your different thoughts.....after you do the exercise we will try to recognise where each thought cam from and how was serving you?**

The life Rules for a permanent happeniss here and now: self-love guidance

Love yourself the way you like to be loved.

Travel others, as you would like to treat.

Do your best in everything that you do. (Do you know that you are doing your best.

It comes through the inner conversations with your soul and your intuition).

**To achieve self-love you have to have those ingredients and practice them in auto pilot all the times.....but in this program I will explore them link to your work role and responsibility as human being we are:.....pretending that you have gained the self-love and you implement the self-love ingredients towards supporting others through the work you do.**

1-Have a vision of how you want to help and how your contribution will support others

2-Be curious when things don't go the way you want ....look beyond what is presented

3-Be determent to be committed to what you agree with yourself.....to practice purity in order to maintain the inner happiness and to explore ways how to implemented into your work

4- Believe in yourself even when things are difficult .....purity is powerful and has deep meaning with it

&5-Love through desire your goals and purpose.......keep loving and just love

&6-Be creative ....creativity brings solution without breaking the law and always finds the way to implement the right thing ....even when you can't see way out....Be creative through using intuition guidance

&7- Be flexible.....never say "I don't have time" but look for the love in you ....there is time for everything you feel right to do....time works for us ....use it

&8-Alloy yourself to be who you want to be.......keep being you even when everyone around you see you as weird .....keep being you if it feels right to you

&9-Don't judge yourself, but be understanding towards yourself.....we all do mistakes ...it's ok ....learn and move on.....do your best not to repeated

&10-Show compassion to yourself....always put yourself number one .....only this way you can support others through your work

&11-Experiment new things and unknown ways if it resonates with you......YES AND YES.....because that is the way of growth and creating new ways for better results .....learning is the way forward ....best learning comes through life experience

12-Have discipline how to stick to your plans, kep daily, weekly, monthly an long term plans .......have time alone to reflect about work you do daily .....that's the way you grow and improve

13-Be genuine.....straightforward and never change .....this is quality of love language....helps you to maintain in higher energy

14-Look for justice towards yourself and your actions towards others......every time you have a shake feeling....stop and reflect...ask intuition for clarification and guidance how to do the right thing and be in the right path ....in path of pure love and permanent happiness

15-Stop being the victim but find ways how to notice the good things you have ...  focus on good things and be aware of things you don't like....you are not alone ....creator is with you all the times and loves you exactly how you are .....is there as a friend, as a therapist and for any conversation you need to talk about ......use it ....

16-Be prepared to keep daily diary.....it will help to see your self in a mirror

17-Willing to put yourself first......never feel guilty for looking after yourself with out hurting others ......in the end of the day this is your life ....enjoy it

🦋 18-Willing never to do to others what you don't like others to do to you......daily reflection is so important .....it does help you to see your day as a movie and notice things that you could not noticed before .....and ask intuition everyday if you did wrong to anyone in the day and if yes ....explore how could you make it better....

🦋 19-Take responsibility for your actions and your happiness.....be responsible.....that is the only way to enjoy your work and help others through your daily work....

🦋 20-Willing to learn to be master of observing what is happening around you daily.....to stay in higher energy so you will be able to observe yourself and others beyond what is happening.....can see in more depth vision ...even what is not said or what could be done to get the results you aim

🦋 21-Create affirmations based on facts that you believe within.......daily should write your affirmation and encourage others around you through your work .....Personalised real affirmations are very powerful

🦋 22-Willing to listen to yourself and only you to be in charge of your decisions and actions.....remember "we are very powerful adult because of the power we have to make decisions" ....use it wisely ....

🦋 23-Make notes daily what you learn from others and your daily experience.....share it with your good friends, supervisions or people that you trust .....the language of energy is powerful ....

24-Willing to have daily conversations with yourself using techniques that you and only you create them and feel comfortable…learn to have it anytime you need it ….even when you physically are working ….practice is everything ….

25-Daily give love to yourself and make note of what you did……loving yourself maintain the inner happiness and the balance of inner world with outside world …..

26-your worries, fears, anxiety, insecurities, or any other emotions that you are experiencing have to be having daily conversation with your inner love in order slowly to turn into love and preparation for resilience on what to get more from this journey of life.

27-Make time for you …..alone time……daily, weekly, and for holiday alone once a year ….

28-Keep distance from people who don't make you happy or distract you from your goal and your purpose……listen to your intuition and never daubt your intuition ….work on recognizing your inner voices

29-Ask for help if you need it……even if we don't get help …still we should ask ….then again come back to ourselves and intuition ….

30-Whatever you do daily pay attention ….to learn, to enjoy it, to understand it, to appreciated, to accepted, to make changes if need it, to be grateful for you are and what you do, be your own critic,

be open to listen to yourself if guidance are need it to change what you did not like, find out what inspired you, to be pure love and just notice anything thing that you notice.

"Remember the reason you are in this life is to enjoy life and the only way to enjoy life is to connect to your pure love that you are born with and shine through the journey of life"

Always staying in the presence of your intuition when you are working in order to be able to give 100% of your best and get an amazing results with lots of love and happeness with out feeling tired or everloaded. This happens through the following two points as starter and then working on magical module:

1- Spending time at least 30min up to 2 hour a day with yourself. At least one day a week should be for you only. (When you are reflecting, that is your soul's voice. Analysis, with knowledge and answers to your questions are coming from the intuition – the voice of creator). But remember, creator never makes decisions for you but is like a therapist to you. You are only provided with answers to your questions. Sometimes, you are not given answers because it is not time yet, or maybe you need to learn something in the meantime. Give 3 examples from your work role that you have been using a similar approach and how that has turned out and what did you get from it?

2- Surround yourself with people whom speak to you the truth through love.
Is food for your self-love and guide you. Also spend time where you feel you can clean and recharge your energy....such as nature, art, writing, good friends, family, children, work, home etc.

297

Fill up below the flower petals with examples of how you appliment point 2 into your life style?

Relationships can effect our personal and work life.

**Be aware of relationships we alloy and have:** The difference between soul-relationship, attraction-relationship, good-relationships and the right relationships need to be understand and aware as that can complicate things and unbalance your self-love. To be able to understand the human first you have to undrstand yourself and developed your listening skills towards the whole you and intuition.

**Exercise:** how do you apply what we just said to the each of the points below:

🦋 Relationship with yourself (what is your relationship to your soul?, how is your romantic relationship on scale 1 to 10 and if is not 10...what do you need to do to make it 10?, Describe your understanding of your soul, intuition, mind, heart and body? How do you notice each of them in daily selftalk?

🦋 Relationship with others around you ....(give an exmple at work challenge where you were able to notice each voice of yourself and what did you gain from it?)

🦋 Relationship with your family... (we know is a deep reason why we hav the family we have ....because is part of our growth....tell me 5 challenges that you still are working on link to family relationship...explain your working plan and 5 challenges that you already have overcome.....for each one share one wisdom you have learned)

👐 Creating the right one in order to get the right one ...(are you the right one? List 7 things that you like to improve on yourself link to relationship topics and list 11 great qualities that you already have).

*Soul relationship is when you only connect through soul but don't agree with each other's actions and thoughts. Human relationship is when you know each other very well including mind, heart and as whole. To be able to recognise those two types of relationship you have self-love first and understanding of universal love then you ar ready for relationship.*

Because we are born with self-love and as we grow we lose it through the influence of others and reality we atomically start running out of love and as our human being is made to function from love we crave for love in others. There are people who love with mind (these love is compromised but is no passion). This is not true love. Some people love with heart. It's like dependence. Sometimes it happens to us that we fall in love firstsight, which means that it falls directly to the soul of the person, but what happens. But what happens? If that person does not live guided by the soul all the time, but lives with the mind and heart then is not the person who you are falling in love with. If that person is not one with his/her soul, that person is not true to themselves as it follows the mind and heart. When we focus only on the soul of a person, we may be blinded to their mind and heart as we see only the good things on that person.

*True love. It is when we fall in love with the soul of the person and has created the life based on the soul guidance, so mind and heart are means that serve their soul.*

299

*So we have to look at as the whole. The mind and heart must be combined to a level with the soul. Same strategy goes for people we work with .....we have to raise our awarness in order to understand others in deep level.*

The difference between the soul and the creators is that the creator has wider knowledge, but the knowledge of the soul comes from knowledge of your life purpose and previus life experiences. Do we need to know how to recognize our soul, starting from the very essence of his existence? Through the spirit we can change our thoughts and leave behind those we do not need. How can we allow the spiral of the spirit to guide us, given that the soul is close to creator, innocent and always right. Also the soul heals the heart as the heart collect feelings from thoughts of mind also. Feelings want more time than thoughts to leave behind (this period lasts 3 months, which happens if you have learned the techniques from previous experiences or have a mentor - about 1 year out of your time practicing with yourself to see stability). Once stability has been achieved, this stability must be maintained and this work depends on person and is unique. For this one needs a prepared mentor. The body is a biological aspect through the body showing signs of lack of love, or things that can be scientifically proven. Thinking in the brain also affects the production of hormones. If the thought is negative, the cells are going to be negative energy, if positive then there is positive energy. Negative thinking occurs when the moment does not feel as it comes. While positive is when you feel and live the moment as it comes and if you cry, every thought is positive if you enjoy the moment, to create the future and to become the best person you have the opportunity to do. If the foundation is based on these three points, thought is called positive.

Thinking that is not based on these three points is negative or harmful to the body and to the person.

### Relationship with others prefesionals:

Relationships is part of universal love. If a person has not achieved self-love, then they will follow their path because they need universal love and they will be dependent on universal love. Universal love is simply survival but nothing else, so survival in the wrong way, breathing without realizing why you are and what is your path and why you really exists. If you do not find self-love you end up hurting others and your self. If you win your love for yourself, then your life becomes meaningful, and you enjoy life, then you can understand and enjoy the love you share during at work. You will be able to understand the other as whole and help to operate from pure love ....because your higher level of energy is able to help with their higher energy and help the other to feel their higher energy. Thats why is important as prefessional to have gained the slf-love in order to be able to help the other to feel your energy levels and wants guidance how to continue to be conected with their true self. If you have not gained the self-love you will be operating in lower level of mind and heart where is no pure love and then you will end up hurting yourself and the other.

### Self-love in my theory is:

Someone who values themselves (it means accepting who you are and allowing yourself to think and plan, in order to be the best you can be), respects themselves (it means in any situation you should respect the idea of acknowledging your feelings, listening to yourself, and liking your qualities, actions, and achievements.

301

Even if you think you don't like your qualities, you must still respect yourself and allow yourself to change those particular qualities), listen to yourself (make time to sit down alone and have a conversation, this could be; an evaluation of the day, reflection on certain situations or caring for your emotions, changing your thoughts/actions, or just saying nice things to yourself and praising yourself for any achievements), caring (caring is a very important word, as you need to care for yourself as you are looking after a baby or a child), allow yourself to dream and be the best you can be (it means setting yourself high standards so you can fulfill your goal and dreams, then making plans on how you're going to make it happen. Don't give up on your dream just because it needs time or hard work. If you truly believe in your dream and want to make it a reality, it is worth the time and effort on order to make it happen).

**My skills are as follows.....and I think every professional should have it in order to achieve the aim of this program.....everyone has the ability to have those skills below....**but the individual can discover after have gained self-love…. (I gained these skills after becoming a product of pure love and finding the urge to see others around me happy, as it did not make sense that I was a product of love alone while others suffering around me. I asked the creator to give me the skills to help others and I had to be creative to know exactly what I required):

1- I connect with your soul (to know who you really are and what your purpose in life is) (This can be achieved through conversations with you), and feeling the energy of your soul, mind and heart…. the energy of whole you.

You can .....tell me qualities that you have similar .....list minimum 5....and 6 that you are working on or you like to gain....

2- I Understand who you are ... who you have become because of your life experiences...what has made you like that ... (through sessions we can discuss all that and understand it together ... to see if you like who you are or need to change in order to get what you want)... You can .....tell me qualities that you have similar.....list minimum 5....and 6 that you are working on or you like to gain....

3- I have a deep understanding of your actions.... Are they created to survive? Are all actions based on your survival mechanism? I can help you to let go of your survivor mechanism so you can be able to enjoy life and not feel the need to survive. We are not here to survive but to enjoy life, this is the main purpose of the creator and you can prove it after you achieve your self-love. It is only when you have achieved self-love that you'll be able to see things clearly.... You can .....tell me qualities that you have similar.....list minimum 5....and 6 that you are working on or you like to gain....

Remember: We all have a gift to serve us in our purpose we have choose to follow.....but first we have to learn how to make ourselves permanent happy all the times here and now.....while we are clear about work we need to do on our future vision.

# Methods are through seven stages of the magical module:

**MOMENTUM**
**ACCEPTANCE**
**GOAL**
**INSPIRATION**
**COMMITMENT**
**AFFIRMATION**
**LOVE**

 **MOMENTUM**

According to David Hawkins everything has an energy vibration; people, places, things, emotions.

This stage is about connecting with your inner power, loving yourself, and writing your own life and making it happen. This is the chapter where all our bad or good experiences will happen; and if you are able to connect with your soul, inner self, and our creator, you will experience the magic of the moment, your blessings and you'll learn how to use your magic to create more magic around you. But if you cannot connect, then ask for help as you will be stuck

in a continuous circle, unable to move onto the next chapter in your life. Open your heart and mind to the universe and try to recognise your true self (your soul), so you can get unlimited information back to you and become the master of your own life.

All the stages are linked and interconnected which means each client went through an individual and flexible journey, based on my skills and what the client offered at the moment. For details of each clients journey and on the work which has been done, refer to chapter seven of the book "Life is Magical…You are Magical". The methodology is fairly general and provides self-guidance for the reader, in order to help them achieve self-love. For more information of this stage can look at main course or mentoring program.

"Success is to finding a way to be content in the present and having a clear vision of your desired future journey. Flexibility is a factor which contributes to success … it is a part of growing and becoming wiser and wiser everyday, as a product of pure love"

### Exercise: Being Present – Preparing yourself for introduction to Mind, Heart, Body and Energy
.....

 1- The energy of the babies

 2- Abilities of children

 3- Power of adult

**The energy of babies** is pure and the reason is pure is because we are created from purity in order to come to this life with free will and free choice to create our life journey.

**Exercise** on discussion/sharing experiences /explaining the difference between purity of the babies and different ages of children and adults......

**Abilities of children** are unlimited; they have great creativity and vision to do so much. Children are great guidance for adults and they come up with solution for everything because their intelegjence is based on energy of babies'. (This point can be explained in depth in stage of acceptance, affirmation and inspiration)

*Exercise: Point out all the good qualities children have and the inner strength they show in different situations.......what you think about their higher intelligence .....have you tried to give them difficult questions to answer or challenging tasks to do ? if yes please lets discuss it in groups their inner power that shines through their intelligence and how can we encourage it to be expanded in their every day life in order to support their wellbeing......also think about the time you were full of higher energy as a child and lets write down your thoughts about it ......*
*At least lets create a strategy how to remind yourself that inner power.....minimum come up with three affirmations for yourself and three other affirmation how to be the best you can be in the job role you are doing.....*

*Power of adult is huge because they have the power of choice and they are the one who can make final decision. (This point is explained in depth through goal, commitment and love stage in the main course of MM).*

306

People have to learn to focus on loving vibrations of babies, rather than hate vibrations of adults, or lower vibrations of mind and heart, if you are focussing on what people have done to you, or what they did and focussing on the negatives that is low vibrations, as long as you give those things credence you are allowing yourself to feed into it, and you create the very things you are trying to avoid. People and things can only be given as much power as you allow because you are a master of your own life by using the adult's power. The power of making decisions on how you will react to outside world and your inner world.

Now coming to your job role !!!

**Exercise:** How your power affects other people's life? Can you make a list of positive impacts and negative impacts that are out of your hands and you can not do more ….but you wish you could do more

After you done the list in two parts then lets make another lists of possibilities that could be done in your wish list if you had more time and power…describe what power you need and how you will be using it….please think like you have all the time in the world you need…..

If you shift your focus on what you can do based on those three points I mentioned and concentrate on what others are doing just as lessen or to stimulate your creativity of your power, you will shift the power and will be operating from higher vibration. In love and divine light.

The language of love is the language of babies that it continues on the stages below:

1-Language of energy

2-Language of body language

3-Language of words

Language of energy
Soul is part of our inner world....part of creator....

Keep the balance:

1- To understand it ...and know exactly why it is important and how it works .....list down 7 strategies that you use to connect with yourself as whole and understand yourself in deep level daily

2- Identify how to discover yourself, which techniques or methods work for you, as we are all different and required individual, tailored methods.....list down 7 strategies and reason why you use them ....

3- How to keep practicing self love (I do it daily, weekly, monthly and yearly .... a holiday alone)...give 7 examples for daily, weekly, monthly and yearly.

# You, Mind, Purpose, Heart, Love

**You: Can make huge difference in your job role**

In this session it is important to be in the moment in order to raise awareness of all the feelings you are unloading. My main focus is establishing a connection to the soul and creator, so that the client experiences energy within their soul. This in turn brings the focus to that feeling for few seconds, as the feelings are mixed with thoughts from the mind and feelings from the heart. During this session it is important to tailor the exercises around the questions below and to the clients individual situation. The importance of these exercises it that they help the individual search for answers, as they are under the influence of their soul. Your higher energy state that we discussed in babies energy helps you to have sharp effective listening skills towards your intuition and others around you to read them in depth for the purpose you need to support them through compassion and understanding.....through the language of love.

**Reminder of your Purpose** can help you to be focused and not get distracted on the thing that does not serve your purpose. This is about you; what you want, where you are at the moment and what actions you have taken so far to accomplish your goals and move closer towards what you want. What can be done? Where should you start? So the work is centered around those questions.

**Heart:** We have to be aware of our feelings, observe, reflect and show compassion and understanding.

309

These are your feelings which are truly sensitive and interact with our job role if we have not found a strategy how to look after them. We have to show love, care, be active listeners all the times in our job role. We also need to be reflective and analyse others feelings and the emotions they may experience in order to have full understanding of what is going on with the person we are supporting.

**Love:** We have to work with our understanding of the individual link to love. We then subsequently bring these ideas into the bigger picture regarding how we want to help. We explore the role of others in your life and allow ourselves to be observers of their thoughts and feelings.

The role of others in your life is important, particularly when you don't have self-love and rely heavily on being loved by others (universal love or passionate love).

That survival mechanism is costing you your happiness and keeping you away from your true self. Therefore, by exploring the role of others and raising awareness of the link between self-love, universal love and passionate love, you finally become familiar with your true self and understand the importance of knowing yourself first in order to be able to understand others and provide the right support.

"By accepting yourself and being fully what you are, your presence can make others happy." (Jane Roberts)

*Understanding how our Mind works and how we can look after it in order to serve "us"...the higher energy we maintain after gaining self-love*

？ How we process information......give 7 examples how you process information from outside world and inner world

？ How we store information....give 7 examples how you store your information's and when do you use it ....why do you store them...

？ How we collect information ...give 7 examples and explain why do you collect them

*The process of reprogramming your mind takes a minimum of six months after you have connected to your true self (the soul) and you are practicing self-love. When you work with your mind you have to raise the awareness of all your thoughts including those, which you have repressed. This can be achieved through various techniques, which are tailored to meet the individual's needs. The steps are simple and the techniques include; spending time alone, making notes, having deep conversations with yourself that lead to a decision and attending coaching sessions at least once a month in order to reflect on your techniques and the methods that you are using. You become a master of your mind while caring for your thoughts through the process of reprogramming them. Thoughts have incredibly great power if we are not connected to our true self and if we create our reality based on our thoughts. On the other hand, if we are connected with our true self and still allow our thoughts to interfere in our life, it will create conflict which results in confusion and leads to various emotions.*
*If these emotions are not a product of love then they could result in physical illness.*

311

"Self-love requires you to be honest about your current choices and thought patterns and undertake new practices that reflect self-worth."
(Caroline Kirk)

"First of all, a soul is not something that you have. It is what you are."
(Jane Roberts, Seth Speaks: The Eternal Validity of the Soul)

It is very important that you listen to your inner child when trying to get the other 20%. Your inner child reminds you to have fun and to stay in touch with the imagination you once had that lead you to be here. This imagination is the epitome of the 20% as it's all about being creative and unique.

This is all about self-love. Therefore we need to love ourselves how we deserve to be treated. We are all kings and queens and we must treat our sacred selves as well as you treat any human on this planet. We must not out everyone's needs ahead of our own as that could causes complications in the future, because we fail to meet our needs as human and we won't function at our best to serve others.

## ACCEPTANCE

Acceptance is a very important stage as you need to have lots of conversation with yourself through the love you have within that we have explained and gone through on momentum stage. Through the conversations you will learn a lot about the power of pure love, the power of the moment, the power of the time and how to share love and care and help others.

"Your purpose is actually quite simple, it's to look deep into yourself, into your soul, and your childhood memories can help you to do that. To discover and nurture, who you truly are, to know and love yourself at the deepest level and to guide yourself back home when you lose your way. The more you do this, the more aware and present you become, which creates more harmony in your life… Your self-worth has nothing to do with your craft or your calling and everything to do with how you treat yourself. Loving and accepting ourselves even when we fail miserably because love is what can heal anything and guide you to feel fulfilled and loved"

" As long as you look for good on you .....your universe will be your teacher "

"When you try to follow the purity you will never feel alone or out of purpose. ..."

" The change comes through your reflection of the conversation you have as whole you by being still. ....by sitting on your energy humbled in universe"

" The universe is everything and can be used in bad way or good way ....only the difference is that negative energy can never give you peace and love but the good energy will give you peace, love and fulfilments. ......... (the God, the religion are just roots to lead you to one direction. ...to understand universe. ...to understand how to use the universe as we have free will and free choice. ....to choose the good energy or the negative energy and is up to us which one we feed on us .....based on what we feed the energy the reality will be created and our feelings. .....the feelings have power for good or bad)".

### Exercise: Home work

Two things to work this month:

    1- To heal/care/love for your heart.....have free time with yourself and be mindfulness about how your heart is feeling, listen, understand it, care for it and show compassion....make notes as through understanding your heart /feelings you will be able to understand the outside world better and learn new things how to do more on supporting others through your job role

2- Create affirmation to grow your confidence and believe in yourself example "I love ... (say your name) because...., I am very confident that I can deal with any situation, no matter what it is , I believe in myself , I can achieve my dreams, I have done (this) and (that) and I am proud of myself....."........

## GOAL

To understand who you are at the present and to be conscious of the choices you make, you must ensure that you have a goal. Dream your wishes, visualize your dreams, and break up them in small goals.

We all wants wealth, health, fame, success, love, peace, harmony, to be surrounded by people who love us, to have the job we love to do and be happy, however, we all have to start with a vision, a plan, decisions, time scales, an action and starting point.  We discussed momentum and acceptance and now we have a clearer idea about how to make the right decisions for ourselves and how to support others that relay on us. This stage is about helping the client reflect, analyse, create and strengthen their connection with their soul/mind/heart/body, in order to obtain the reality they desire. If we are able to be a good role module that defenitly we can do a great job on supporting those who relay on us.

**Exercise :** Self displine is very important quality. Lets make a list of what self-despline is and what it requires to mantain it .....how we can reflected in our job role ? The soul knows no limitations, describe in your understanding why the soul does not know limitations and why we use the word "can't"? How would you implement in your work?

314

**Remember:** The soul "we" have both free will and free choice. Our choices, actions, decisions and influences the decisions of karma and law of life that creats the reality. Self love>universal love>passionate love (intimate love).

-Self love (is believing in yourself, accepting yourself and where you are, taking time to understand yourself.

-Being a great holistic facilitator to yourself (to question, to criticize, to discipline, empathise, love, care, to be kind, be understanding, a shoulder to cry on, be encouraging, treat your self, respect, forgive, remind yourself to live in the moment, help to follow the plan 80% and 20%).

-Allowing yourself to be a unique version of yourself, find yourself by spending time
with the whole you (soul, mind, heart and body).

### Believe in yourself

You can believe in the creator, but how can you believe in life, the universe and the creator if you don't believe in yourself?

What does it mean to believe in yourself?

How can we discipline ourselves to take the journey to achieving self-belief? (An exercise with small steps which leads from the place the individual is currently at to the place they want to be in self love...to be in a workbook as an exercise).

## Goal exercise link to your work role:

-Goal road or map exercise on self-love

-On top of this exercise to be the reason what is the whole purpose of them loving themselves?

-Where that will take them and how ? In detailed plan journey from where they are and where they want to go.

"love yourself from the source of the soul and not from the ego of the overflowing cover of the diaphanous" …..how would you implement it?

"Doing bad to others is enough even thinking about it, and it will come back to you what you do….even twice" …..how would you explain and implemented through your work?

"Its not integrity others to save your life because you have to do it as it is your lessons and everything lies within you…be creative, curios and determent to create your own path"

As you are in that energy can you create 11 cards with the answers from you of the points below please so you can have it and remind yourself anytime you feel the need too:

1- For knowledge. .   do you feel wiser and why? You are smart and why ?

2- Trust … how do you know how to believe?

3- Practicing self-confidence and self believe.... how?

4- Practicing God's Faith/will/guidance

5- Daily plan, weekly and monthly plan...how can you?

6- How can you practice emptiness of Your Mind and letting go

7- How to reach the space, the universe?

8- The imagination of things that happen tomorrow ... how would you like to go tomorrow or the situation that will occur and how can you adjust it on your best interest? Based on pure love?

9- Weekly prayer or gratitude.

10- How could you learn from others?

11- How
to protect yourself and enjoy the flow of moment

*Walking on straight line towards purity, only the one who is determined to walk straight and is enthralled with the real listening can do.*

## Food for your goal:

1- love

2- eating healthy

3- having faith in your self

4-comonicating with your self

5- Spending time alone / daily / weekly / holiday.

6-Spending time where you love and feel good.

7- Spending time with people who you feel yourself.

8- Having your heart and mind free.

9-Treat yourself.

10- Tell others how you feel.

11- Remembering this is only and only your journey, your life.

**Exercise:** This list may change but for me right now that's what it is my soul food. What is yours?......create your own list ….

## INSPIRATION

Don't forget to pause and notice the amazing things and the blessings around us. This enables you to become inspired from anything that surrounds you, bad or good. You'll always have something to spark your inspiration and fire your creativity.

**Exercise:** give 7 examples for each topic below and explain the reason you are using those inspiration and why you have listed the way you have…..

 What does inspiration mean to you?

 Think about how inspiration helps your day to day life?

Think about who does inspire you and why/how?

Do babies inspire you and how/why?

How can you be inspiration for others…..create a list …

How can you be more inspirational in your work place?

Why do you think is important to be inspired and to be inspiration for others?

## COMMITMENT

Be a good listener and listen to your inner guidance, nature, and all your senses. Trust the universe. Give time and flow with time by being spontaneous in order to understand when the time is right to do what you need to do.

### Commitment /explore

Techniques and methods to stay committed

Have a goal in mind/visualisation

Wake up with your goal in mind and go to sleep with the goal in mind/imagination/no limitation /respect limitations/doing good to yourself and others

Truly believe that it is a possible to achieve the goal you already gone through the stage of the goal/believe in power of purity/how important is to maintain self-love….the harmony of peace

319

# Commitment exercise

**Drawer Exercise** - it involves organising your thoughts, goals, priorities, and responsibilities. We also need to be aware of the following; self love, purpose, food for the soul, karma, upholding your values and principles....and how do those qualities help you in your work role? What can you do different now that you are at this stage of MM?

**Life Ladder Exercise-** You can replace the ladder with any object of your choice, however what is important it going through every steps of the ladder while also keeping in mind the language of love we talked about regarding self-love and implementing at work place.

## AFFIRMATION

Tell yourself how good you are. Remind yourself of all the amazing things you are doing and the great abilities you have to help yourself and others.

### Affirmation/ Exercise

What are affirmations?

These are ways we:

Support .....tell me more how do they support you with your work?

Discipline .....how do you use it through your work?

How do you use them at work?

Do you discipline yourself when necessary? Why?

Do you offer yourself emotional support? ....give example

How do you help others through affirmations?

What is the difference between the powerful affirmation and week affirmation?

Give example

**The Affirmation stage work also involves co-working with the individuals.**

**Benefits of keeping a daily diary are below:**

1-Someone to listen to you without judgment but with pure love.

2-Someone to give you advice as you write your free thoughts, automatically you will be connected to your inner child and your soul.

3-For someone to cry with and feel sympathy and empathy with you.

4-For someone you can discuss any confusions with.

5-For someone to laugh with at your stupidity and foolishness.

6-Someone to help you analyse and reflect on your mistakes/actions/experiences/painful moments /good memories etc.

7- After you finish the writing you can decide how to use your notes to help others if you want too....

# LOVE

Love yourself and everything on this earth to attract the love energy that leads to you living in a magical world. Love is the medicine of life and the place where you get your answers

***Love exercise:*** *list 7 examples for each point …..and use the colors next to each point to describe the feelings or meaning you like to give ….or can draw something or put a name …*

How can we give the right love to others ?

How can we embrace the love of life?

Create poem about love for yourself and life

Make a plan on how to keep your self-love and how to contribute to create a world of peace and love through your work

## Love

Love yourself, life, others, and everything that surrounds you … this is the meaning of life … this is the disappearance of dissatisfaction … this is the disappearance of complaints … this is the love without limitations …. free love ….magic love that creates magic on you and the life you are surrounded.

I do believe everyone is unique and special.

We are not here in this world to be better the others but to be product of love and help those who has not achieved it yet to be product of love.

Is important to understand the order of love: self-love, universal love and passionate/intimate love.

You can search throughout the entire universe for someone who is more deserving of your love and affection than you are yourself, and that person is not to be found anywhere. You yourself, as much as anybody in the entire universe deserve your love and affection."
— Buddha

### 1-Treat others the way you like to be treated:

-In order to know what is best for others first you have to know what is good for you and for that reason you have to have self-love to know yourself well and to feel loved in order to help others on their needs.

People who have self love they know the answer to this question but for those who don't have self love you have to raise your awareness on those points below before you get involved on with others or interact with others as you will end up hurting yourself and others:

Before you process the though its on your head consider how is helping the other? How do I know it's really helping the other? What is the length time my help will last and what they will do after that? What is costing me to help others? Can I find a way that can help them to help themselves in long term? If I was on their place what I really wanted? And take deep breath before getting the answer or best is before you ask the question to yourself as it allows you to connect to your true self and listen to the true answer instead of the ego answer. In my understanding from my self-discovery the ego is the mind created based on thoughts that takes us easy options and just thinks for themselves

323

and never consider the other best interest. The true self is the soul, the pure energy link directly to creator and that is all about helping you to be pure to yourself, which that leads automatically to be pure to others. The ego, the part of mind that is fulfilled with information and guidance how to gain things (things such as , money, love , affection, attention, fame, life style to show off ect)only for your self that is not pure because you will hurt others for your interest, such us lie, manipulate, physically hurt others, steal, emotionally hurt others and lots more that you may think off or seen around. If you manage to see the difference between the pure thought and ego thought than you have started the first step of practising on treating others the way you like to be treated. Remember if you have not achieved the self love then you will not know how to treat yourself and you are lost on ego which you notice as you don't feel fulfilled, loved and complete exactly where you are and you need help before you start to help others or think you can help others as you are effected by your ego and need healing through your soul.

The self love will help you to link to your purest side, which is your soul and then you will treat yourself with pure compassion and understanding and you will know how to treat others.

Do your best in everything you decide to do:
Doing your best means working hard to discover and achieve self love, which is the key to fulfilment, peace and love. Self-discovery sets the foundations for an enjoyable life in which you are fulfilling the purpose of your existence. A number of the qualities include: - create - Analyze options - choose the options – – look for justice - love - diplomacy - sharp observation - work- simplicity - wish - plan - a short and long vision for the future - dedication - reflection - decisions - purpose - and the magic of love is to love yourself and you life, the way you want to and not how others impose.

**Exercise:** Take each point the ingredients of knowing if you are doing your best in your work place and link it to your work place. Give two examples how you are implementing it and two more how could you do more... think about three guidance of universe that we discussed above...

Few tips for some prefessions to remind them how powerful their role is on contributing to creating a world of love and peace:

**Parents/foster carers/social workers** have most important role in the world because they are looking after the new generation....if they gain the self-love automatically they will be able to raise a generation that have self-love......which mean the world already is in peace and love.

Few tips how MM can support you and children by exploring topics below:

How to listen to the child? Pay attention to the points below through your intuition, pure love language and their lower energy:

School behaviour

Silence    Misbehaviour

Walking    With you    Eating habits

Child's favourite TV programmes and hobbies,

Playing with others and alone    With strangers

## You can help and support their wellbeing

Experiencing different emotions and being balanced.

**Teaching children the self-love guidance.** Helping them to build a trusting and committed relationship with themselves and universe.

**Momentum:** (is important stage for you and the child to face the self life journey through eyes of pure love).

**Acceptance:** (is important stage as by accepting here and now can make peace with the self and have a deep conversation where want to be and to do with the life journey).

**Goal:** (is important as with out direction the child is lost and don't move nowhere or may waste time going for wrong goals....guiodance are important blended with healthy options, boundaries and life consoquences) .

**Inspiration:** (is the fuel that keeps the child going and reminding why they love the goal, themself and their life journey).

**Commitment:** (it is healthy and important to look after commitment plan as that is the way gives you caurage to keep going and to help be fulfilled, in peace and love .....and to move towards your future vision flexibilities).

**Affirmation:** (this part is all about showing appreciation to your self and the child, telling your self how much you value and here it comes critics also for both ....you and the child in order to acsept everything, to change and grow).

**Love**: (we all want to be loved so this is the whole point of being here in this life, being loved by yourself, by your family, by friends and others, by partner and sharing love with yourself, others and universe.....need to keep reminding our selves self-love and support the wellbeing of the child by implementing the istrument of self-love).

Looking at this quote below from Albert Einstein it seems clearly that there are people before me who have had the same idea and understanding of the life and the bridge that link to spiritual world. But even in the quote it says is not possible but I will challenge that it is possible. I have achieved it, so few clients have achieved and few others are fully aware of the process and they are practising it, and most of the clients have started to believe that it is true and can be achieved as they have achieved small steps towards the process. I know 100% that can be achieved but as I have explained the ingredients you need to uncover within and practice it through those main three guidance on question one in questioners through empowering reflection and openings, but how many will have a go, that only time will tell.

'A human being is part of the whole, called by us "universe," a part limited in time and space. He experiences himself, his thoughts and feelings, as something separate from the rest -- a kind of optical delusion of consciousness. This delusion is a kind of prison for us, restricting us to our personal desires and to affection for a few persons nearest to us. Our task must be to free ourselves from this prison by widening our circle of compassion to embrace all living creatures and the whole of nature in its beauty. Nobody is able to achieve this completely, but the striving for such achievement is in itself part of the liberation, and a foundation for inner security.'

*Albert Einstein:*

"Self discovery journey is link to your life path purpose.....and it will be reviewed with clear outlook in the time between death and rebirth....."

### Self discovery have few stages:

**Stage one:** to make yourself happy here and now with everything you choose to do .....as we do have choice how to react to outside world ...

**Stage two:** learning how to maintain that contentment achieved on stage one .....

**Stage three:** exploring in more depth your life purpose .....how to make use of yourself better? How to contribute to loved ones around you? .....what are your abilities?....explore your gifts ....

**Stage four:** get our self out there and test your abilities.... test what you decided to do from stage three ...

**Stage five:** retreat yourself in more deep self discovery and get all in .......be one with universe and have a deep chat where you want to go ....what is your next step ....evaluate your self discovery and life path.....choose what makes you happy here and now.........as you continue fulfilling your life purpose....

**Stage six:** don't know yet as I have not reached it yet ....but I know it is stage six and stage seven......or could be up to stage eleven.....

Discovering yourself always rewards you with the stability to handle yourself in times when circumstances keep you trapped.

This is a gripping journey of Self-discovery across continents and lifetimes that shows you how to get clear about what makes you happy, what your life purpose is and changes required to be the best version of yourself.

Not everyone has the same path to finding the inner Self but sometimes experiencing the journey of another does lay the path for you to set you off towards your destination.

**LOCAL AUTHORITIES/FOSTER AGENCIES/SOCIAL WORKER/THERAPIST AND ALL THE OTHER PROFESSIONALS THAT ARE INVOLVED IN CHILD'S LIFE CAN BENEFIT FROM MM.**
**FEW SUGGESTIONS HOW TO SUPPORT THE WELL BEING OF CHILDREN IN CARE:**

Exercise/strategies/methods can be explored in depth if it is requested and all together can make those suggestion below happen:
Time scale is from one year up to three year training to get the results this programme aims for......which is to help the professionals and children to gain self-love....to be happy here and now all the times and contribute to a world being in harmony of pure love.

Boundaries/consequences to be firm and clear.....through the language of love we explored. Establish strong, clear boundaries, keeping very firm boundaries that may not be breached. This is all part of the structure that children require and is fine line between being controlled by the child.....Use natural (or life) consequences used with nurturing....language of love.

330

 Have Structure, routine, firm boundaries, understand cause of exhibited behaviours, Identify child's triggers ASP in order to give the right support to the child. Accept the child as a product of pure love and understand their behaviour…..in order to have success here in three months you have to be happy here and now all the times as an adult looking after the child who has gone through a traumatised experience ….

 All healthy options should be discussed with the child and allow the child to be part of the decision ……but each option should be explored properly where it takes the child….in order the child to be fully aware of what they are taking responsibility for and what they are going to aspect.

 Nice energy - grounded/centred just like what you're talking about to be encouraged for support in order the child to progress towards their well-being and enjoy life here and now…….this should be provided by all the adults who are part of the child.

 Through the support that is provided the child one step at the time can work with their triggers more and more and finding healthy ways to navigate the emotions towards pure love…..self-love.

 The TRANSITIONS in children in care is their life experience …….I think very easier can be prevented by working all of us together and not just taking easier option to move the child because the child wishes, or want too, or has complained and investigation has not taken place yet, etc ……before you move the child the new placement has to be assessed properly and the old place in mean time  …..also we have to be firm with the child to explore responsibilities, boundaries,

consequences, and where each topic will lead the child.......as we can see so many cases the children are master of manipulating the system because that's the only way they feel in control......and don't want to look forward but only how to go back to their parents or survive where they are ......this state is not healthy for well-being of the child....... things need to be explored and find a better way how to really support children in care ....not just follow the system ........this easier can be done if they were more people who have achieved the self-love.....who practice in auto pilot the self-love ingredients. Sometimes nothing happens and children are left for long periods of time feeling lonely. A transition so small like going to school can send the children into a state of dysregulation and fear. The person who has gained self-love will go extra miles to do their job properly because is their passion to do the job they have choose to do......will never have excuses for not having enough time. That's why is so important us as professionals to work on ourselves to gain self-love we talked about. You understand the nature of things on an intuitive level. People included, which allows for greater compassion and magical results.

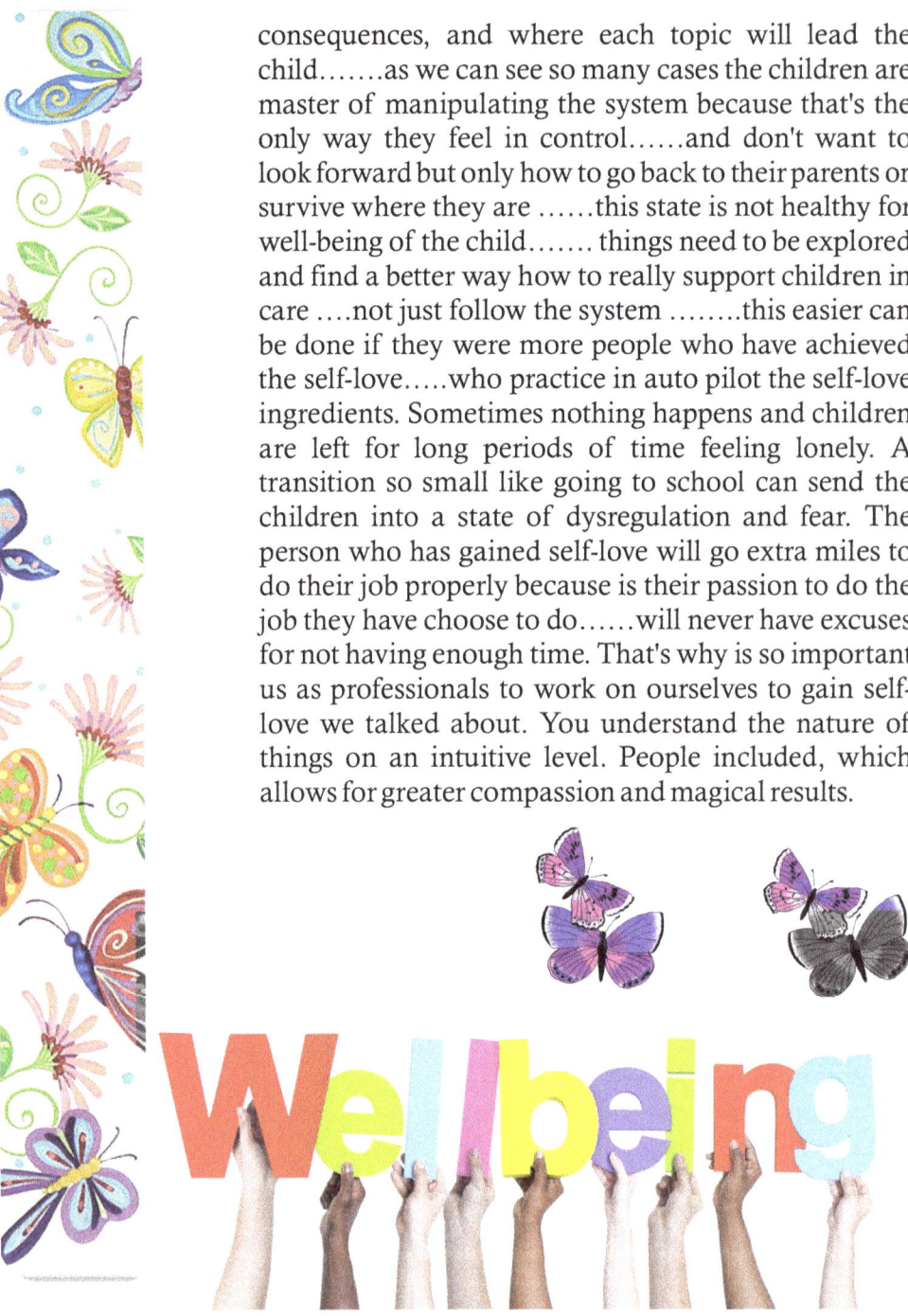

332

# POLITICIANS!!!!!!!!

If Politicians had gained self-love …..the world would be running differently

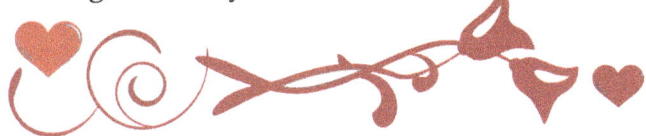

POLICE!!!!, INVESTIGATORS!!! , SCHOOLS/TEACHERS!!!, THERAPIST!!!, SCIENTIST!!!, HEALERS!!!, SOCIAL WORKERS!!!,… MAYBE MORE …

If individuals who work on those roles would have gained self-love …….I am 100% sure the world would be different and lot much better place where children will enjoy growing up with full passion for life ……where adults will appreciate little things and the beauty of life and would have so much love to share with each other instead of complaining and hurting themselves and others in the journey searching for happiness in outside world……when they should search in their inner world.

 ## Including business

Content- outcome- income- process- people- environment - clients - daily reflection- maybe changes- reflect on changes- conclusion - plan- action - and again start from reflection the process.....based on human role in this earth and our duty to enjoy life and what we do ....

Effectiveness of implementing employee mental health and well-being strategies to improve productivity and performance need a new approach,
here is why.

The healthier your employees are, the more control they have over their job. They know how to clarity of what is expected of them, their team members and their customers. The better your employees' feel, the better they perform. Employees who are present and feel more grounded does the job properly and is willing to grow everyday through challenges life presents. The more aware your employees are, the more productive they can become providing their sense of personal purpose is in alignment with the company's one. Self-love is the passion to life and everything that surrounds us. Training on self-love is need it in any area of our life in order to get the results we want, to understand and help others and contribute to a peaceful/loving world we all want to be .......**LIFE IS MAGICAL**....YOU ARE MAGICAL....ACT AND LIVE

Who am I? and how did I come up with the idea that permanent happiness is here and now and it is within us through practising purity and working with ourselves.......and why?

I am "An Individual who loves herself, others and life and want's to see the world in peace and love since I was age seven years old"

Sister    Psychotherapist    Friend

Degree on Psychosocial Studies    Daughter

Author

Mother    Counsellor

Foster Carer    Personal Coach

Educational Coach

Life Investigator to Bring Solutions

Youth Coach

Teacher of Language of Love    Healer

Philosopher Since Age 7 Years old

Researcher to Found the Causes of Pain /Truth Behind What is Presented

The title and the subtitle of this book explain exactly what is about the book and we all know the word "purity" but don't believe in power of it.

Therefore I explained on my first book my self-discovery since age seven year old where I asked creator for the world to be loved and filled with love.

The book is called "A magical Life"

In my second book I have done research to validate my theory based on pure Self-love as being the key to a fulfilled, meaningful life and is paramount to creating peace and love where you are. It is only when you have fully embraced self-love that you have developed a clear and flexible plan for your future. The methods used in this study are based on the seven stages of the magical module, closely intertwined with a therapeutic approach. Comprising self-love and therapeutic skill, the methodology was applied to 30 clients aged between six and sixty. Participants in the study came from a variety of backgrounds and faced a range of diverse issues. The research consisted of 50 questionnaires, containing 11 questions each and further observation via social media. The results were overwhelming and at first glance indicated that all the participants were both unhappy and lacking self-love. Further analysis of the results revealed that individuals were in survival mode for universal and passionate love, which create the foundations for further issues such as suicide, crime, abuse and loneliness. These in turn become a driving force behind destructive and harmful behaviours such as materialism, casual sex simply for the excitement without loving commitment, drug consumption or a failure to achieve childhood goals and visions. A number of clients with whom I worked very closely with, developed a holistic approach, which was based on the magical module. These individuals developed a depth of self-love over time, which has transformed their view of both themselves and their life, making way for inner harmony, peace and love. They then possessed the ability to reflect these new found feelings to the outside and into their reality.

The ultimate purpose of this book is to present you with all the tools and inner resources needed to turn your life around and to help you discover the pure love which you have subconsciously been searching for, but for so long have been unable to understand or achieve.

The book tittle is "Life is Magical…You are Magical"

At this link below you will find the book to read it for free on block/article button www.holisticmagicalapproach.com

**References of the research done on the book "Life is Magical…You are Magical"**

1) Huss. B. (2014). Spirituality: The Emergence of a New Cultural Category and its Challenge to the Religious and the Secular. Journal of Contemporary Religion. Volume 29, Issue 1. P47-60.

2) Albaugh, J.A. (2003)'Spirituality and life-threatening illness: a phenomenological study',Oncology Nursing Forum, 30: 4. P:593-598.

3) Kotsos, T. (2017). Self-love the greatest love of all. Mind Your Reality. Change the Invisible and the Visible will Follow. Available online at: <http. http://www.mind-your-reality.com/self_love.html>

4) Department of Health. (2011). Spiritual care at the end of life: a systematic review of the literature. Available Online at: <http://www.dh.gov.uk/publications>

5)Jones, R.A., Taylor, A.G., Bourgignon, C., Steeves, R. Fraser, G. Lippert, M. Theodorescu, D., Matthews, H & Kilbridge, K.L. (2007). Complementary and alternative medicine modality use and beliefs among African American Prostate Cancer survivors. Oncology Nursing Forum, 34: 2, 359 364

6)Marie Curie (2009). Liverpool Care Pathway for the dying patient (LCP) Pocket Guide. Liverpool: Marie Curie Palliative Care Institute.

7)Department of Health (2009) End of Life Care Strategy First annual report, London: DH Publications.

8) Nardella, N. (2014). Why Self-Love is the Most Important form of Love. Available Online at: < https://www.elephantjournal.com/2014/10/why-self-love-is-the-most-important-form-of-love-natalie-nardella/>

9)Koenig, H.G., McCulough, M.E. & Larson, S.S. (2001) Handbook of Religion and Health Oxford: Oxford University Press.

10) NICE. (2015) New guidelines on end of life care. National Institute for Health Care and Excellence. Available online at: <https://www.nhs.uk/news/medical-practice/new-guidelines-on-end-of-life-care-published-by-nice/>

11)Coyte, M.E., Gilbert, P. & Nicholls, V. (2007) Spirituality, Values and Mental Health: Jewels for the Journey, London: Jessica Kingsley.

12) Elliot D. Cohen Ph.D (2012). What Would Aristotle Do? Are You Your Own Person?
Take the Self-Determination Inventory to Find Out. Available online at https://www.psychologytoday.com/blog/what-would-aristotle-do/201202/are-you-your-own-person

13) Adamson M (2017). Connecting with the Divine. The major world religions and their beliefs about God. Hinduism, Buddhism, Islam, Christianity, and New Age. Available online at < https://www.everystudent.com/features/connecting.html>

14) Frater J. (2007). Top 10 Organized Religions and their Core Beliefs. Available online at < http://listverse.com/2007/07/31/top-10-organized-religions-and-their-core-beliefs/>

15) Rich T. (2011). What Do Jews Believe? Level: Basic. Available online at http://www.jewfaq.org/beliefs.htm
16. Steinberg M. (1965). Basic Judaism. The essential book for Jews and non-Jews eager to know more about one of the world's great religions. P:6.

17. Views on Heaven and Hell. Available online at: https://christianity.org.uk/index.php/a/views-on-heaven-and-hell.php

18. Moberg D. (1984). Subjective Measures of Spiritual Well Being. Review of Religious Research. Religious Research Association. New York.

19) Steiger N. & Lipson J. (1985). Self Care Nursing: Theory and Practice. Brady Communications, Bowie, Maryland.

20) Freeman. J (2014). 7 levels of consciousness: The path of enlightenment. Transcendental Meditation. Available online at: < https://tmhome.com/books-videos/7-states-of-consciousness-video-interview/>

21) Stoll R. (1979). Guidelines for spiritual assessment. American Journal of Nursing. 79(9),1574-1577.

22) Howden J.W. (1992). Development and psychometric characteristics of the spirituality assessment scale. Unpublished doctoral dissertation, Texas Woman's University, Denton, Texas.

23) Frankl V.E. (1959). Man's Search for Meaning. Washington Square Press. Washington.

24) Oldnall A. (1996). Meeting the spiritual needs of patients. Journal of Advanced Nursing. 23:138.

25) Burkhardt M. (1989) Spirituality: an analysis of the concept. Holistic Nursing Practice 3(3), 69–77.

26) Culliford. L. (2017). Spirituality and Art. A priceless living bridge between mind and spirit. Spiritual wisdom for secular times. Avalilable online at: https://www.psychologytoday.com/blog/spiritual-wisdom-secular-times/201712/spirituality-and-art

27. Camic PM. Playing in the mud: health psychology, the arts and creative approaches to health care. J Health Psychol 2008;13(2):287–298

28. Stuckey. H.L. and Nobel. J. (2010). The Connection Between Art, Healing, and Public Health: A Review of Current Literature. American Journal of Public Health. 100(2): 254–263.

29. Jusino. T. (2017). Mayim Bialik Explains How Science and Religion Can Co-Exist. Available online at: https://www.themarysue.com/mayim-biyalik-science-religion-co-exist/

30. Dietrich. E. (2017). Is Science a Religion? Available online at: https://www.psychologytoday.com/blog/excellent-beauty/201710/is-science-religion

31. Lovgren. S. (2004). Evolution and Religion Can Coexist, Scientists Say. Available online at:https://news.nationalgeographic.com/news/2004/10/1018_041018_science_religion.htm

32. Greene. B. (2005). The Fabric of the Cosmos: Space, Time, and the Texture of Reality. Penguin Press.

33. Mastin. (2011). Arguments for Atheism. Living without religion with a clear conscience. Available online at: < http://www.argumentsforatheism.com/what.html>

34. www.oxforddictionaries.com

35. Kipp. M. (2014). Daily Love. Growing into Grace.

36. Merritt, Anna Lea. Love Locked Out: The Memoirs of Anna Lea Merritt with a Checklist of Her Works. Boston: Museum of Fine Arts, 1981.

37. Bandura, A. (1986). Social foundations of thought and action: A social cognitive theory. Englewood Cliffs, NJ: Prentice Hall.

38. Schunk, D. H. (1999). Social self-interaction and achievement behavior. Educational Psychologist, 34, 219-227.

39. Hardy, D. (2012). A Seven-Step Prescription for Self-Love. Self-love is an action, not a state of feeling good.

**"Power of Pure Love..." Educational Book
is based on Holistic Spiritual Approach
on Magical Module to help others to understand
that "Practising Purity Teaches you Self-
Love...Permanent Happiness and Contribute
to Creating a Peaceful
and Loving World ".**

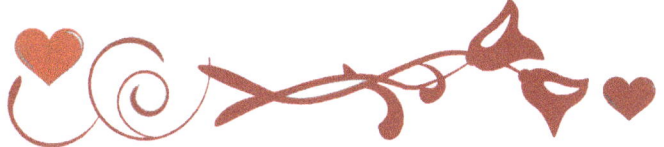

Based on that aim are created the seven programs how to live a peaceful and loving life here and now: Gain self-love, take action based on guidance of your true self, learn how to live a life guided by your soul and intuition and learn how to keep balance of your whole you (mind, heart, body, soul and intuition).

**Benefits** of those achievements are to overcome any illness, trauma, difficulties, relationship confusions, loneliness, be the best you can be in your job, help others in right direction, suicide thoughts, self-harm, addictions, achieving your full potential and basically anything that you are struggling or getting on the way of being happy, fulfilled and loved here and now.

**Note:** Who copy my methods will just make their journey harder as it can not be taught by person who has not gained self-love (be guided by their soul and intuition) ....and the person who has gained self-love will never copy because they will have their own unique way of contributing to the world .... and to sharing with others their wisdom ......

**In order to teach Magical Module you have to be trained by Holistic Spiritual Magical Approach Module.**

*Exercise template*

*Life Map*

Who
are
you?

# Answers

www.ingramcontent.com/pod-product-compliance
Lightning Source LLC
Chambersburg PA
CBHW051506120626
46551CB00012B/794